Stewardship

—

A Counter-Formation Guide

Table of Contents

Introduction

Why Counter-Formation?

First, we are constantly being formed. We are far more subject to being influenced than we think. We are not static beings. The environment we live in, what we read and watch, the relationships we engage in, where we go and what we do, are always shaping our desires, our beliefs, and our habits. We are dynamic beings who are always being formed, whether we realize it or not. We can either be formed towards the way of Jesus, or formed away from it. In previous generations, it was common for people to become Christians after inheriting a vast reservoir of Christian teaching. The Christian story had shaped and influenced the institutions in which people were formed. But now people are often unfamiliar with the Bible and unsure of what it means to be human. "Right and wrong" is increasingly determined by what "feels" right or wrong.

Second, the rate of deformation is staggering. In this digital age, technology collectively assaults us with deforming ideas. Technology can be a tool for the common good, and it can be used to spread the good news of Jesus and form people towards him. But we are in an unprecedented moment in human history where each of us are constantly plugged in, constantly consuming, constantly connected. We are continually being fed versions of "the good life" that are usually not true or beneficial. We are surrounded by stories of heroes and villains that unconsciously shape our beliefs. Those subtle stories, those versions of "the good life," are twisting our desires and forming us in directions that are not ultimately for our good.

Third, formation is never passive. Counter-formation will require grace-fueled effort. If we think we can simply float through life and effortlessly become more like Jesus, we are gravely mistaken. The rate of deformation we experience has gone from a lazy river to a raging rapid that is sweeping us off our feet. Increasingly, we have seen people tire of swimming against the cultural current, leading to their departure from the Christian faith. Without thoughtful effort, without new habits, and without true community, we will be swept away by the current. But deformation is neither inevitable nor guaranteed. With the help of the Holy Spirit, we can stand firm against the forces pulling us away from Jesus. By God's grace, we can work to have a life constantly shaped by the way of Jesus. In our age of deformation, we don't have to panic about the darkness of the world. Rather, we trust that Jesus is still at work, transforming his people by his grace.

What Does Counter-Formation Look Like?

I appeal to you therefore, brothers, by the mercies of God, to present your bodies as a living sacrifice, holy and acceptable to God, which is your spiritual worship. Do not be conformed to this world, but be transformed by the renewal of your mind, that by testing you may discern what is the will of God, what is good and acceptable and perfect.

Romans 12:1-2

This passage speaks to us about both deformation and counter-formation. When Scripture says, "Do not be conformed to this world," it is describing deformation. It is warning us against being conformed to the values of the world, the loves of the world, the desires of the world, and the versions of "the good life" that the world presents to us. In contrast, it invites us to "be transformed by the renewal of your mind." This is counter-formation. It is encouraging us to embrace the transforming work of grace—which comes to us through various means in order to shape what we love, believe, and do.

We cannot respond to deformation by recreating an idealized version of the so-called "good old days." Nor can we kick the can down the road and hope that someday discipleship and mission will become easier. Rather, we must renew our minds and present our bodies as living sacrifices. To do that, we must name some of the most significant forces of deformation in our culture today. We have to recognize what these voices are saying and where they are leading us. But that cannot be all. We must also hear and receive what God is telling us. Jesus came to bring better news than anything this world has to offer. We need our minds, our hearts, and our imaginations to be shaped by that good news.

Counter-formation will require us to practice and renew habits of formation—both alone and together. We must study and cultivate historic Christian virtues that have fallen out of favor in the broader culture. We must pursue and prize powerful encounters with God—in all of his truth, goodness, and beauty. By the mercies of God, counter-formation is both possible and worth fighting for together.

How to Use This Counter-Formation Guide

The mission of Frontline Church is multiplying gospel communities that love God, love people, and push back darkness. Our community groups are one of the primary places we live out that mission. This Counter-Formation Guide contains four trainings you can work through together as a community group every two weeks—either in family meals or in discipleship groups. Each session will include a brief Bible discussion, a ten-minute teaching video, discussion questions, and an exercise. The training videos can be accessed at *frontlinechurch.com/formation*.

Most of our community groups follow an "alternating weeks" format, with a family meal on the first and third week of the month, and discipleship groups on the second and fourth week. If your group follows that format, you can work through these trainings in eight weeks (e.g., four consecutive discipleship groups, meeting every other week).

In addition, this Counter-Formation Guide contains 40 daily liturgies for you to work through individually over the course of those same eight weeks. There are five daily liturgies a week, designed to be used as an aid to your time of individual devotion. Each daily liturgy contains a brief call to worship, two Scripture readings, a prayer of confession and assurance, a benediction, and a blank page for notes. The whole process is designed to take no more than fifteen minutes. If you fall behind in any given week, don't feel the need to make up the missed days.

How Should We Think About Consumerism?

How Should We Think About Consumerism?

Call to Worship

As you begin, have someone pray this prayer out loud for the group.
This prayer is based on James 1.

Father of lights, every good and perfect gift comes from you. Your generosity knows no bounds and never changes. In your grace, you gave us life by the Word of truth. Today we ask for wisdom to know how to live as stewards of your gifts—remembering that you give generously to all without reproach or reservation. *Amen.*

Bible Conversation

Have someone read the following Scripture and discussion question out loud.
Spend up to 5 minutes in discussion.

Bless the LORD, O my soul,
and all that is within me,
bless his holy name!
Bless the LORD, O my soul,
and forget not all his benefits,
who forgives all your iniquity,
who heals all your diseases,
who redeems your life from the pit,
who crowns you with steadfast love and mercy,
who satisfies you with good
so that your youth is renewed like the eagle's.
Psalm 103:1-5

▶ *According to this passage, what good gifts does God give to his people? What*
should be our response to these good gifts?

Training Notes

Watch the video entitled "How Should We Think About Consumerism?" found at *frontlinechurch.com/formation.* Use the notes below and fill in the blanks to follow along with the video.

Our enormously productive economy demands that we make consumption
our way of life, that we convert the buying and use of goods into rituals, that
we seek our spiritual satisfactions, our ego satisfactions, in consumption...
We need things consumed, burned up, replaced, and discarded at an ever
increasing rate.
Victor Lebow, *Journal of Retailing*

God is a _____

> Then God said, "Let us make man in our image, after our likeness. And let
> them have dominion over the fish of the sea and over the birds of the heavens
> and over the livestock and over all the earth and over every creeping thing
> that creeps on the earth." **Genesis 1:26**

God actually wants us to enjoy what he has created and to enjoy the gifts he has
given. Our God is a Father who delights in giving and sharing.

> I perceived that there is nothing better for them than to be joyful and to do
> good as long as they live; also that everyone should eat and drink and take
> pleasure in all his toil—this is God's gift to man. **Ecclesiastes 3:12-13**

Our Loves are Profoundly _____

> To be human is to be on a quest. To live is to be marked on a kind of
> unconscious journey towards a destination of your dreams... You can't not bet
> your life on something. You can't not be headed somewhere. We live leaning
> forward, bent on arriving at the place we long for.
> **James K.A. Smith,** *You Are What You Love*

Our hearts reveal our deepest longings, desires, and beliefs about life.

> But what comes out of the mouth proceeds from the heart, and this defiles
> a person. For out of the heart come evil thoughts, murder, adultery, sexual
> immorality, theft, false witness, slander. These are what defile a person...
> **Matthew 15:18-20**

We were designed to love God first and most, and to love his gifts second.

> Put first things first, and we get second things thrown in: put second things
> first, and we lose both first and second things.
> **C.S. Lewis,** *The Collected Letters of C.S. Lewis*

We are Called to be _____

> What is man that you are mindful of him, and the son of man that you care
> for him? Yet you have made him a little lower than the heavenly beings and
> crowned him with glory and honor. You have given him dominion over the
> works of your hands; you have put all things under his feet. **Psalm 8:4-6**

God has not called us to live our lives as consumers that cling to his gifts. But he
has called us to be stewards, to receive these gifts as a sacred trust, and to use
them in ways that honor his goodness.

Exercise

Set a timer for five minutes. In the space below, each of you should write down as many gifts from God in your life that you can think of until the time runs out. You might include material goods, hobbies, relationships, necessities, talents, or circumstances. Think outside the box and include anything that seems like a gift. After this exercise, discuss the questions on the facing page.

God's Good Gifts

Discussion

▶ *Were there any things that surprised you? Were there things you never thought of as a gift before? If so, what were they?*

▶ *Look over your list. Do you generally relate to these things as gifts from God or as substitutes for God? How would you steward these things differently if you received each one of these things as a gift from God?*

Benediction

To conclude your time, pray this prayer out loud together. The following is based on 2 Thessalonians 2:16-17.

Now may the Lord Jesus Christ himself, and God the Father, who loved us and gave us eternal comfort and good hope through grace, comfort our hearts and establish them in every good work and word. *Amen.*

Daily Liturgies: Week 1

———

Stewards of God

Stewards of God

Call to Worship

An invitation from God to all humanity to behold and join the story, work, and eternal worship of Jesus. This prayer is based on Hebrews 2 and 4.

Jesus, you are a merciful and faithful high priest, crowned with glory and honor. You took my punishment, in my place, and graciously tasted death for me. You brought many sons and daughters to glory through suffering. Through death, you destroyed the one who has the power of death. Who am I that you are mindful of me and that you care for me? In this moment, give me confidence to draw near to your throne of grace, that I might receive the mercy and help I so desperately need. *Amen.*

Psalm 2

Why do the nations rage
and the peoples plot in vain?
The kings of the earth set themselves,
and the rulers take counsel together,
against the LORD and against his Anointed, saying,
"Let us burst their bonds apart
and cast away their cords from us."

He who sits in the heavens laughs;
the Lord holds them in derision.
Then he will speak to them in his wrath,
and terrify them in his fury, saying,
"As for me, I have set my King
on Zion, my holy hill."

I will tell of the decree:
The LORD said to me, "You are my Son;
today I have begotten you.
Ask of me, and I will make the nations your heritage,
and the ends of the earth your possession.
You shall break them with a rod of iron
and dash them in pieces like a potter's vessel."

Now therefore, O kings, be wise;
be warned, O rulers of the earth.
Serve the LORD with fear,
and rejoice with trembling.
Kiss the Son,
lest he be angry, and you perish in the way,

for his wrath is quickly kindled.
Blessed are all who take refuge in him.

Confession

A call to acknowledge and forsake sin against God and one another.

Jesus, you loved the unlovable. You feasted with the broken and the immoral. But I confess that, though I'm called to follow you, I often withdraw my presence and withhold my love from those around me. Father, forgive me. *I confess that I am not my own, but belong to you.*

Jesus, with all your strength, you sought to offer goodness to the world and glory to your Father. But I confess that I often withhold good from others and only seek to glorify myself. Father, forgive me. *I confess that I am not my own, but belong to you.*

Silently reflect on the ways you have strayed from God's gracious authority. Confess aloud and receive God's free grace through Jesus.

Assurance

An invitation to receive the assurance of a new identity in the finished work of Christ.

Lord, even though I have sinned against you, still you have loved me and given yourself for me. My old self went to the cross with Christ. And now it is no longer I who live, but Christ who lives in and through me. I am no longer my own, but I have been bought with an unspeakable price—your very blood. Your Spirit lives in me and leads me to lay aside my weak desires for the deeper delight of living for your glory. I have been made for you, I have been bought by you, and now I belong to you. *Thanks be to God!*

Scripture Reading

The surrender to God's good and authoritative Word.

The words of the preacher, the son of David, king in Jerusalem.

Vanity of vanities, says the Preacher,
vanity of vanities! All is vanity.
What does man gain by all the toil
at which he toils under the sun?
A generation goes, and a generation comes,
but the earth remains forever.
The sun rises, and the sun goes down,
and hastens to the place where it rises.
The wind blows to the south

and goes around to the north;
around and around goes the wind,
and on its circuits the wind returns.
All streams run to the sea,
but the sea is not full;
to the place where the streams flow,
there they flow again.
All things are full of weariness;
a man cannot utter it;
the eye is not satisfied with seeing,
nor the ear filled with hearing.
What has been is what will be,
and what has been done is what will be done,
and there is nothing new under the sun.
Is there a thing of which it is said,
"See, this is new"?
It has been already
in the ages before us.
There is no remembrance of former things,
nor will there be any remembrance
of later things yet to be
among those who come after.

Ecclesiastes 1:1-11

Prayer

An invitation to bring the needs of our bodies, hearts, and minds to the care of God.

Offer prayers for yourself and for others.

Benediction

A blessing from the authority of Scripture spoken over the people of God.
The following is based on 2 Thessalonians 2:16-17.

Now may the Lord Jesus Christ himself, and God the Father, who loved me and gave me eternal comfort and good hope through grace, comfort my heart and establish it in every good work and word. *Send me now into the world as a steward of your good gifts.*

Stewards of God

Call to Worship

An invitation from God to all humanity to behold and join the story, work, and eternal worship of Jesus. This prayer is based on John 1.

Jesus, you are the Word of God. In the beginning, you were with God, and you were God. All things were made through you; nothing was made without you. You are life, and you bring light to our dark hearts. You took on flesh and dwelt among us so we might finally see and know the Father. Open my eyes to behold your glory, glory as of the only Son from the Father, full of grace and truth. *Amen.*

Psalm 6

TO THE CHOIRMASTER: WITH STRINGED INSTRUMENTS; ACCORDING TO THE SHEMINITH. A PSALM OF DAVID.

O LORD, rebuke me not in your anger,
nor discipline me in your wrath.
Be gracious to me, O LORD, for I am languishing;
heal me, O LORD, for my bones are troubled.
My soul also is greatly troubled.
But you, O LORD—how long?

Turn, O LORD, deliver my life;
save me for the sake of your steadfast love.
For in death there is no remembrance of you;
in Sheol who will give you praise?

I am weary with my moaning;
every night I flood my bed with tears;
I drench my couch with my weeping.
My eye wastes away because of grief;
it grows weak because of all my foes.

Depart from me, all you workers of evil,
for the LORD has heard the sound of my weeping.
The LORD has heard my plea;
the LORD accepts my prayer.
All my enemies shall be ashamed and greatly troubled;
they shall turn back and be put to shame in a moment.

Confession

A call to acknowledge and forsake sin against God and one another.

God of all grace, you have given me your Spirit and commissioned me as the aroma of Christ on earth. But I confess that I have taken your presence for granted and sought to satisfy my own cravings before looking to the needs of others. *Father, my heart is prone to wander.*

You have created me for relationship, but I have pulled away from my neighbors. I have lived like an island and pretended to be self-sufficient. I have believed the lie that it is more blessed to receive than to give. *Father, my heart is prone to wander.*

Silently reflect on the ways you have strayed from God's gracious authority. Confess aloud and receive God's free grace through Jesus.

Assurance

An invitation to receive the assurance of a new identity in the finished work of Christ.

While I was still a sinner, you died for me. Jesus, you were resurrected so I could know true and abundant life. While I have loved imperfectly, you have loved perfectly. While I have withheld myself from God and others, you have given yourself fully to the world. Lord, you intercede for me today, and you promise not to leave me as I am. Even now, you are at work to form me into your image, from one degree of glory to the next. You have not finished what you began in me, and you will not give up until it is done. *Thanks be to God!*

Scripture Reading

The surrender to God's good and authoritative Word.

I the Preacher have been king over Israel in Jerusalem. And I applied my heart to seek and to search out by wisdom all that is done under heaven. It is an unhappy business that God has given to the children of man to be busy with. I have seen everything that is done under the sun, and behold, all is vanity and a striving after wind.

What is crooked cannot be made straight,
and what is lacking cannot be counted.

I said in my heart, "I have acquired great wisdom, surpassing all who were over Jerusalem before me, and my heart has had great experience of wisdom and knowledge." And I applied my heart to know wisdom and to know madness and folly. I perceived that this also is but a striving after wind.

_____

For in much wisdom is much vexation,
and he who increases knowledge increases sorrow.

Ecclesiastes 1:12-18

Prayer

An invitation to bring the needs of our bodies, hearts, and minds to the care of God.

Offer prayers for yourself and for others.

Benediction

A blessing from the authority of Scripture spoken over the people of God.
The following is based on 2 Corinthians 13:14.

May the grace of the Lord Jesus, the love of God the Father, and the fellowship of the Holy Spirit go with me today. *Send me now into the world as a steward of your good gifts.*

Stewards of God

———

Call to Worship

An invitation from God to all humanity to behold and join the story, work, and eternal worship of Jesus. This prayer is based on Psalm 50.

O God, you are the Mighty One who summons the riches of the earth with a word. The world and its fullness are yours. To you belong the cattle on a thousand hills, and even the sparrows rest in your care. You need no one and lack nothing, yet you command my praise—for your glory and for my joy. When my hands are full, fill me with gratitude. When my hands are empty, satisfy me with yourself. *Amen.*

Psalm 8

TO THE CHOIRMASTER: ACCORDING TO THE GITTITH. A PSALM OF DAVID.

O LORD, our Lord,
how majestic is your name in all the earth!
You have set your glory above the heavens.
Out of the mouth of babies and infants,
you have established strength because of your foes,
to still the enemy and the avenger.

When I look at your heavens, the work of your fingers,
the moon and the stars, which you have set in place,
what is man that you are mindful of him,
and the son of man that you care for him?

Yet you have made him a little lower than the heavenly beings
and crowned him with glory and honor.
You have given him dominion over the works of your hands;
you have put all things under his feet,
all sheep and oxen,
and also the beasts of the field,
the birds of the heavens, and the fish of the sea,
whatever passes along the paths of the seas.

O LORD, our Lord,
how majestic is your name in all the earth!

Confession

A call to acknowledge and forsake sin against God and one another.

Jesus, you warned me, "Where your treasure is, there your heart will be also."

For all the ways I have given myself to the riches of this world—forgive me and bend my heart back to you.

For all the ways I have shut my eyes to the needs of the poor—open my hands to be generous like you.

For all the ways I have preferred your blessings over your presence—change me that I might enjoy your gifts and treasure you as Giver.

For all the ways I have looked to money as my security—save me from false refuges and help me to lean on you.

Silently reflect on the ways you have strayed from God's gracious authority. Confess aloud and receive God's free grace through Jesus.

Assurance

An invitation to receive the assurance of a new identity in the finished work of Christ.

Father, you are a generous Giver. There is no good thing that you withhold from me, for it is your good pleasure to give me the kingdom. You did not spare your own Son, but gave him up for us all. Surely you will graciously provide for my every need, both now and forever. If you are for me, who can be against me? You have given me the Spirit of adoption and called me your child. Who is there to condemn? Nothing in all creation will be able to separate me from your love. *Thanks be to God!*

Scripture Reading

The surrender to God's good and authoritative Word.

I said in my heart, "Come now, I will test you with pleasure; enjoy yourself." But behold, this also was vanity. I said of laughter, "It is mad," and of pleasure, "What use is it?" I searched with my heart how to cheer my body with wine—my heart still guiding me with wisdom—and how to lay hold on folly, till I might see what was good for the children of man to do under heaven during the few days of their life. I made great works. I built houses and planted vineyards for myself. I made myself gardens and parks, and planted in them all kinds of fruit trees. I made myself pools from which to water the forest of growing trees. I bought male and female slaves, and had slaves who were born in my house. I had also great possessions of herds and flocks, more than any who had been before me in Jerusalem. I also gathered for myself silver and gold and the treasure of kings and provinces. I got singers, both men and women, and many concubines, the delight of the sons of man.

So I became great and surpassed all who were before me in Jerusalem. Also my wisdom remained with me. And whatever my eyes desired I did not keep from them. I kept my heart from no pleasure, for my heart found pleasure in all my toil, and this was my reward for all my toil. Then I considered all that my hands had done and the toil I had expended in doing it, and behold, all was vanity and a striving after wind, and there was nothing to be gained under the sun.

Ecclesiastes 2:1-11

Prayer

An invitation to bring the needs of our bodies, hearts, and minds to the care of God.

Offer prayers for yourself and for others.

Benediction

A blessing from the authority of Scripture spoken over the people of God. The following is based on Philippians 4:19-20.

O my God, you will supply my every need according to your riches in glory in Christ Jesus. To you, Father, be glory forever and ever. *Send me now into the world as a steward of your good gifts.*

Stewards of God

Call to Worship

An invitation from God to all humanity to behold and join the story, work, and eternal worship of Jesus. This prayer is based on James 1.

Father of lights, every good and perfect gift comes from you. Your generosity knows no bounds and never changes. In your grace, you gave me life by the Word of truth. Today I ask for wisdom to know how to live as a steward of your gifts—remembering that you give generously to all without reproach or reservation. *Amen.*

Psalm 11

TO THE CHOIRMASTER. OF DAVID.

In the LORD I take refuge;
how can you say to my soul,
"Flee like a bird to your mountain,
for behold, the wicked bend the bow;
they have fitted their arrow to the string
to shoot in the dark at the upright in heart;
if the foundations are destroyed,
what can the righteous do?"

The LORD is in his holy temple;
the LORD's throne is in heaven;
his eyes see, his eyelids test the children of man.
The LORD tests the righteous,
but his soul hates the wicked and the one who loves violence.
Let him rain coals on the wicked;
fire and sulfur and a scorching wind shall be the portion of their cup.
For the LORD is righteous;
he loves righteous deeds;
the upright shall behold his face.

Confession

A call to acknowledge and forsake sin against God and one another.

I hear your call to love you with all my heart, mind, and strength. But I confess that my love for you is diluted—made weak by lesser desires and a divided heart. *I have sought my own way, and my soul is unsatisfied.*

You have called me to steward your creation and fill it with blessing. But I have twisted your good gifts and turned them to my own ends. *I have sought my own way, and my soul is unsatisfied.*

• • • • •

Silently reflect on the ways you have strayed from God's gracious authority. Confess aloud and receive God's free grace through Jesus.

Assurance

An invitation to receive the assurance of a new identity in the finished work of Christ.

Father of lights, you richly give me all things to enjoy. In Jesus, I stand clothed in purity, washed in mercy, and adopted in love. I no longer have to leave the table of the world unsatisfied. You have spread a banquet before me filled with every good thing. Surely goodness and mercy will follow me all the days of my life, and I will find satisfaction in you. *Thanks be to God!*

Scripture Reading

The surrender to God's good and authoritative Word.

So I turned to consider wisdom and madness and folly. For what can the man do who comes after the king? Only what has already been done. Then I saw that there is more gain in wisdom than in folly, as there is more gain in light than in darkness. The wise person has his eyes in his head, but the fool walks in darkness. And yet I perceived that the same event happens to all of them. Then I said in my heart, "What happens to the fool will happen to me also. Why then have I been so very wise?" And I said in my heart that this also is vanity. For of the wise as of the fool there is no enduring remembrance, seeing that in the days to come all will have been long forgotten. How the wise dies just like the fool! So I hated life, because what is done under the sun was grievous to me, for all is vanity and a striving after wind.

I hated all my toil in which I toil under the sun, seeing that I must leave it to the man who will come after me, and who knows whether he will be wise or a fool? Yet he will be master of all for which I toiled and used my wisdom under the sun. This also is vanity. So I turned about and gave my heart up to despair over all the toil of my labors under the sun, because sometimes a person who has toiled with wisdom and knowledge and skill must leave everything to be enjoyed by someone who did not toil for it. This also is vanity and a great evil. What has a man from all the toil and striving of heart with which he toils beneath the sun? For all his days are full of sorrow, and his work is a vexation. Even in the night his heart does not rest. This also is vanity.

There is nothing better for a person than that he should eat and drink and find enjoyment in his toil. This also, I saw, is from the hand of God, for apart from him who can eat or who can have enjoyment? For to the one who pleases him God has given wisdom and knowledge and joy, but to the sinner he has given the business of gathering and collecting, only to give to one who pleases God. This also is vanity and a striving after wind.

Ecclesiastes 2:12-26

Prayer

An invitation to bring the needs of our bodies, hearts, and minds to the care of God.

Offer prayers for yourself and for others.

Benediction

A blessing from the authority of Scripture spoken over the people of God. The following is based on Ephesians 3:20-21.

Now to him who is able to do far more abundantly than all I could ask or think, according to the power at work within me—to him be glory in the Church and in Christ Jesus throughout all generations, forever and ever. *Send me now into the world as a steward of your good gifts.*

Stewards of God

Call to Worship

An invitation from God to all humanity to behold and join the story, work, and eternal worship of Jesus. This prayer is based on Hebrews 2 and 4.

Jesus, you are a merciful and faithful high priest, crowned with glory and honor. You took my punishment, in my place, and graciously tasted death for me. You brought many sons and daughters to glory through suffering. Through death, you destroyed the one who has the power of death. Who am I that you are mindful of me and that you care for me? In this moment, give me confidence to draw near to your throne of grace, that I might receive the mercy and help I so desperately need. *Amen.*

Psalm 16

A MIKTAM OF DAVID.

Preserve me, O God, for in you I take refuge.
I say to the LORD, "You are my Lord;
I have no good apart from you."

As for the saints in the land, they are the excellent ones,
in whom is all my delight.

The sorrows of those who run after another god shall multiply;
their drink offerings of blood I will not pour out
or take their names on my lips.

The LORD is my chosen portion and my cup;
you hold my lot.
The lines have fallen for me in pleasant places;
indeed, I have a beautiful inheritance.

I bless the LORD who gives me counsel;
in the night also my heart instructs me.
I have set the LORD always before me;
because he is at my right hand, I shall not be shaken.

Therefore my heart is glad, and my whole being rejoices;
my flesh also dwells secure.
For you will not abandon my soul to Sheol,
or let your holy one see corruption.

•••••

You make known to me the path of life;
in your presence there is fullness of joy;
at your right hand are pleasures forevermore.

Confession

A call to acknowledge and forsake sin against God and one another.

Jesus, you loved the unlovable. You feasted with the broken and the immoral. But I confess that, though I'm called to follow you, I often withdraw my presence and withhold my love from those around me. Father, forgive me. *I confess that I am not my own, but belong to you.*

Jesus, with all your strength, you sought to offer goodness to the world and glory to your Father. But I confess that I often withhold good from others and only seek to glorify myself. Father, forgive me. *I confess that I am not my own, but belong to you.*

Silently reflect on the ways you have strayed from God's gracious authority. Confess aloud and receive God's free grace through Jesus.

Assurance

An invitation to receive the assurance of a new identity in the finished work of Christ.

Lord, even though I have sinned against you, still you have loved me and given yourself for me. My old self went to the cross with Christ. And now it is no longer I who live, but Christ who lives in and through me. I am no longer my own, but I have been bought with an unspeakable price—your very blood. Your Spirit lives in me and leads me to lay aside my weak desires for the deeper delight of living for your glory. I have been made for you, I have been bought by you, and now I belong to you. *Thanks be to God!*

Scripture Reading

The surrender to God's good and authoritative Word.

For everything there is a season, and a time for every matter under heaven:
a time to be born, and a time to die;
a time to plant, and a time to pluck up what is planted;
a time to kill, and a time to heal;
a time to break down, and a time to build up;
a time to weep, and a time to laugh;
a time to mourn, and a time to dance;
a time to cast away stones, and a time to gather stones together;
a time to embrace, and a time to refrain from embracing;
a time to seek, and a time to lose;

•••••

a time to keep, and a time to cast away;
a time to tear, and a time to sew;
a time to keep silence, and a time to speak;
a time to love, and a time to hate;
a time for war, and a time for peace.

What gain has the worker from his toil? I have seen the business that God has given to the children of man to be busy with. He has made everything beautiful in its time. Also, he has put eternity into man's heart, yet so that he cannot find out what God has done from the beginning to the end. I perceived that there is nothing better for them than to be joyful and to do good as long as they live; also that everyone should eat and drink and take pleasure in all his toil—this is God's gift to man.

Ecclesiastes 3:1-13

Prayer

An invitation to bring the needs of our bodies, hearts, and minds to the care of God.

Offer prayers for yourself and for others.

Benediction

A blessing from the authority of Scripture spoken over the people of God.
The following is based on 2 Thessalonians 2:16-17.

Now may the Lord Jesus Christ himself, and God the Father, who loved me and gave me eternal comfort and good hope through grace, comfort my heart and establish it in every good work and word. *Send me now into the world as a steward of your good gifts.*

•••••

Daily Liturgies: Week 2

———

Stewards of God

Stewards of God

Call to Worship

An invitation from God to all humanity to behold and join the story, work, and eternal worship of Jesus. This prayer is based on John 1.

Jesus, you are the Word of God. In the beginning, you were with God, and you were God. All things were made through you; nothing was made without you. You are life, and you bring light to our dark hearts. You took on flesh and dwelt among us so we might finally see and know the Father. Open my eyes to behold your glory, glory as of the only Son from the Father, full of grace and truth. *Amen.*

Psalm 21

TO THE CHOIRMASTER. A PSALM OF DAVID.

O LORD, in your strength the king rejoices,
and in your salvation how greatly he exults!
You have given him his heart's desire
and have not withheld the request of his lips. SELAH
For you meet him with rich blessings;
you set a crown of fine gold upon his head.
He asked life of you; you gave it to him,
length of days forever and ever.
His glory is great through your salvation;
splendor and majesty you bestow on him.
For you make him most blessed forever;
you make him glad with the joy of your presence.
For the king trusts in the LORD,
and through the steadfast love of the Most High he shall not be moved.

Your hand will find out all your enemies;
your right hand will find out those who hate you.
You will make them as a blazing oven
when you appear.
The LORD will swallow them up in his wrath,
and fire will consume them.
You will destroy their descendants from the earth,
and their offspring from among the children of man.
Though they plan evil against you,
though they devise mischief, they will not succeed.
For you will put them to flight;
you will aim at their faces with your bows.

Daily Liturgy: Week 2, Day 1

Be exalted, O LORD, in your strength!
We will sing and praise your power.

Confession

A call to acknowledge and forsake sin against God and one another.

God of all grace, you have given me your Spirit and commissioned me as the aroma of Christ on earth. But I confess that I have taken your presence for granted and sought to satisfy my own cravings before looking to the needs of others. *Father, my heart is prone to wander.*

You have created me for relationship, but I have pulled away from my neighbors. I have lived like an island and pretended to be self-sufficient. I have believed the lie that it is more blessed to receive than to give. *Father, my heart is prone to wander.*

Silently reflect on the ways you have strayed from God's gracious authority. Confess aloud and receive God's free grace through Jesus.

Assurance

An invitation to receive the assurance of a new identity in the finished work of Christ.

While I was still a sinner, you died for me. Jesus, you were resurrected so I could know true and abundant life. While I have loved imperfectly, you have loved perfectly. While I have withheld myself from God and others, you have given yourself fully to the world. Lord, you intercede for me today, and you promise not to leave me as I am. Even now, you are at work to form me into your image, from one degree of glory to the next. You have not finished what you began in me, and you will not give up until it is done. *Thanks be to God!*

Scripture Reading

The surrender to God's good and authoritative Word.

I perceived that whatever God does endures forever; nothing can be added to it, nor anything taken from it. God has done it, so that people fear before him. That which is, already has been; that which is to be, already has been; and God seeks what has been driven away.

Moreover, I saw under the sun that in the place of justice, even there was wickedness, and in the place of righteousness, even there was wickedness. I said in my heart, God will judge the righteous and the wicked, for there is a time for every matter and for every work. I said in my heart with regard to the children of man that God is testing them that they may see that they themselves are but beasts. For what happens to the children of man and what happens to the beasts is the

——

same; as one dies, so dies the other. They all have the same breath, and man has no advantage over the beasts, for all is vanity. All go to one place. All are from the dust, and to dust all return. Who knows whether the spirit of man goes upward and the spirit of the beast goes down into the earth? So I saw that there is nothing better than that a man should rejoice in his work, for that is his lot. Who can bring him to see what will be after him?

Ecclesiastes 3:14-22

Prayer

An invitation to bring the needs of our bodies, hearts, and minds to the care of God.

Offer prayers for yourself and for others.

Benediction

A blessing from the authority of Scripture spoken over the people of God. The following is based on 2 Corinthians 13:14.

May the grace of the Lord Jesus, the love of God the Father, and the fellowship of the Holy Spirit go with me today. *Send me now into the world as a steward of your good gifts.*

● ＊＊＊＊

Stewards of God

———

Call to Worship

An invitation from God to all humanity to behold and join the story, work, and eternal worship of Jesus. This prayer is based on Psalm 50.

O God, you are the Mighty One who summons the riches of the earth with a word. The world and its fullness are yours. To you belong the cattle on a thousand hills, and even the sparrows rest in your care. You need no one and lack nothing, yet you command my praise—for your glory and for my joy. When my hands are full, fill me with gratitude. When my hands are empty, satisfy me with yourself. *Amen.*

Psalm 27

OF DAVID.

The LORD is my light and my salvation;
whom shall I fear?
The LORD is the stronghold of my life;
of whom shall I be afraid?

When evildoers assail me
to eat up my flesh,
my adversaries and foes,
it is they who stumble and fall.

Though an army encamp against me,
my heart shall not fear;
though war arise against me,
yet I will be confident.

One thing have I asked of the LORD,
that will I seek after:
that I may dwell in the house of the LORD
all the days of my life,
to gaze upon the beauty of the LORD
and to inquire in his temple.

For he will hide me in his shelter
in the day of trouble;
he will conceal me under the cover of his tent;
he will lift me high upon a rock.

And now my head shall be lifted up
above my enemies all around me,

and I will offer in his tent
sacrifices with shouts of joy;
I will sing and make melody to the LORD.

Hear, O LORD, when I cry aloud;
be gracious to me and answer me!
You have said, "Seek my face."
My heart says to you,
"Your face, LORD, do I seek."
Hide not your face from me.
Turn not your servant away in anger,
O you who have been my help.
Cast me not off; forsake me not,
O God of my salvation!
For my father and my mother have forsaken me,
but the LORD will take me in.

Teach me your way, O LORD,
and lead me on a level path
because of my enemies.
Give me not up to the will of my adversaries;
for false witnesses have risen against me,
and they breathe out violence.

I believe that I shall look upon the goodness of the LORD
in the land of the living!
Wait for the LORD;
be strong, and let your heart take courage;
wait for the LORD!

Confession

A call to acknowledge and forsake sin against God and one another.

Jesus, you warned me, "Where your treasure is, there your heart will be also."

For all the ways I have given myself to the riches of this world—forgive me and bend my heart back to you.

For all the ways I have shut my eyes to the needs of the poor—open my hands to be generous like you.

For all the ways I have preferred your blessings over your presence—change me that I might enjoy your gifts and treasure you as Giver.

For all the ways I have looked to money as my security—save me from false refuges and help me to lean on you.

Silently reflect on the ways you have strayed from God's gracious authority. Confess aloud and receive God's free grace through Jesus.

Assurance

An invitation to receive the assurance of a new identity in the finished work of Christ.

Father, you are a generous Giver. There is no good thing that you withhold from me, for it is your good pleasure to give me the kingdom. You did not spare your own Son, but gave him up for us all. Surely you will graciously provide for my every need, both now and forever. If you are for me, who can be against me? You have given me the Spirit of adoption and called me your child. Who is there to condemn? Nothing in all creation will be able to separate me from your love. *Thanks be to God!*

Scripture Reading

The surrender to God's good and authoritative Word.

Again I saw all the oppressions that are done under the sun. And behold, the tears of the oppressed, and they had no one to comfort them! On the side of their oppressors there was power, and there was no one to comfort them. And I thought the dead who are already dead more fortunate than the living who are still alive. But better than both is he who has not yet been and has not seen the evil deeds that are done under the sun.

Then I saw that all toil and all skill in work come from a man's envy of his neighbor. This also is vanity and a striving after wind.

The fool folds his hands and eats his own flesh.

Better is a handful of quietness than two hands full of toil and a striving after wind.

Again, I saw vanity under the sun: one person who has no other, either son or brother, yet there is no end to all his toil, and his eyes are never satisfied with riches, so that he never asks, "For whom am I toiling and depriving myself of pleasure?" This also is vanity and an unhappy business.

Two are better than one, because they have a good reward for their toil. For if they fall, one will lift up his fellow. But woe to him who is alone when he falls and has not another to lift him up! Again, if two lie together, they keep warm, but how can one keep warm alone? And though a man might prevail against one who is alone, two will withstand him—a threefold cord is not quickly broken.

Daily Liturgy: Week 2, Day 2

———

Better was a poor and wise youth than an old and foolish king who no longer knew how to take advice. For he went from prison to the throne, though in his own kingdom he had been born poor. I saw all the living who move about under the sun, along with that youth who was to stand in the king's place. There was no end of all the people, all of whom he led. Yet those who come later will not rejoice in him. Surely this also is vanity and a striving after wind.

Ecclesiastes 4:1-16

Prayer

An invitation to bring the needs of our bodies, hearts, and minds to the care of God.

Offer prayers for yourself and for others.

Benediction

A blessing from the authority of Scripture spoken over the people of God. The following is based on Philippians 4:19-20.

O my God, you will supply my every need according to your riches in glory in Christ Jesus. To you, Father, be glory forever and ever. *Send me now into the world as a steward of your good gifts*

Stewards of God

Call to Worship

An invitation from God to all humanity to behold and join the story, work, and eternal worship of Jesus. This prayer is based on James 1.

Father of lights, every good and perfect gift comes from you. Your generosity knows no bounds and never changes. In your grace, you gave me life by the Word of truth. Today I ask for wisdom to know how to live as a steward of your gifts—remembering that you give generously to all without reproach or reservation. *Amen.*

Psalm 30

A PSALM OF DAVID. A SONG AT THE DEDICATION OF THE TEMPLE.

I will extol you, O LORD, for you have drawn me up
and have not let my foes rejoice over me.
O LORD my God, I cried to you for help,
and you have healed me.
O LORD, you have brought up my soul from Sheol;
you restored me to life from among those who go down to the pit.

Sing praises to the LORD, O you his saints,
and give thanks to his holy name.
For his anger is but for a moment,
and his favor is for a lifetime.
Weeping may tarry for the night,
but joy comes with the morning.

As for me, I said in my prosperity,
"I shall never be moved."
By your favor, O LORD,
you made my mountain stand strong;
you hid your face;
I was dismayed.

To you, O LORD, I cry,
and to the Lord I plead for mercy:
"What profit is there in my death,
if I go down to the pit?
Will the dust praise you?
Will it tell of your faithfulness?
Hear, O LORD, and be merciful to me!
O LORD, be my helper!"

———

You have turned for me my mourning into dancing;
you have loosed my sackcloth
and clothed me with gladness,
that my glory may sing your praise and not be silent.
O LORD my God, I will give thanks to you forever!

Confession

A call to acknowledge and forsake sin against God and one another.

I hear your call to love you with all my heart, mind, and strength. But I confess that my love for you is diluted—made weak by lesser desires and a divided heart. *I have sought my own way, and my soul is unsatisfied.*

You have called me to steward your creation and fill it with blessing. But I have twisted your good gifts and turned them to my own ends. *I have sought my own way, and my soul is unsatisfied.*

Silently reflect on the ways you have strayed from God's gracious authority. Confess aloud and receive God's free grace through Jesus.

Assurance

An invitation to receive the assurance of a new identity in the finished work of Christ.

Father of lights, you richly give me all things to enjoy. In Jesus, I stand clothed in purity, washed in mercy, and adopted in love. I no longer have to leave the table of the world unsatisfied. You have spread a banquet before me filled with every good thing. Surely goodness and mercy will follow me all the days of my life, and I will find satisfaction in you. *Thanks be to God!*

Scripture Reading

The surrender to God's good and authoritative Word.

Guard your steps when you go to the house of God. To draw near to listen is better than to offer the sacrifice of fools, for they do not know that they are doing evil. Be not rash with your mouth, nor let your heart be hasty to utter a word before God, for God is in heaven and you are on earth. Therefore let your words be few. For a dream comes with much business, and a fool's voice with many words.

When you vow a vow to God, do not delay paying it, for he has no pleasure in fools. Pay what you vow. It is better that you should not vow than that you should vow and not pay. Let not your mouth lead you into sin, and do not say before the messenger that it was a mistake.

Why should God be angry at your voice and destroy the work of your hands? For when dreams increase and words grow many, there is vanity; but God is the one you must fear.

Ecclesiastes 5:1-7

Prayer

An invitation to bring the needs of our bodies, hearts, and minds to the care of God.

Offer prayers for yourself and for others.

Benediction

A blessing from the authority of Scripture spoken over the people of God. The following is based on Ephesians 3:20-21.

Now to him who is able to do far more abundantly than all I could ask or think, according to the power at work within me—to *him* be glory in the Church and in Christ Jesus throughout all generations, forever and ever. *Send me now into the world as a steward of your good gifts.*

Stewards of God

———

Call to Worship

An invitation from God to all humanity to behold and join the story, work, and eternal worship of Jesus. This prayer is based on Hebrews 2 and 4.

Jesus, you are a merciful and faithful high priest, crowned with glory and honor. You took my punishment, in my place, and graciously tasted death for me. You brought many sons and daughters to glory through suffering. Through death, you destroyed the one who has the power of death. Who am I that you are mindful of me and that you care for me? In this moment, give me confidence to draw near to your throne of grace, that I might receive the mercy and help I so desperately need. *Amen.*

Psalm 33:1-12

Shout for joy in the LORD, O you righteous!
Praise befits the upright.
Give thanks to the LORD with the lyre;
make melody to him with the harp of ten strings!
Sing to him a new song;
play skillfully on the strings, with loud shouts.

For the word of the LORD is upright,
and all his work is done in faithfulness.
He loves righteousness and justice;
the earth is full of the steadfast love of the LORD.

By the word of the LORD the heavens were made,
and by the breath of his mouth all their host.
He gathers the waters of the sea as a heap;
he puts the deeps in storehouses.

Let all the earth fear the LORD;
let all the inhabitants of the world stand in awe of him!
For he spoke, and it came to be;
he commanded, and it stood firm.

The LORD brings the counsel of the nations to nothing;
he frustrates the plans of the peoples.
The counsel of the LORD stands forever,
the plans of his heart to all generations.
Blessed is the nation whose God is the LORD,
the people whom he has chosen as his heritage!

Confession

A call to acknowledge and forsake sin against God and one another.

Jesus, you loved the unlovable. You feasted with the broken and the immoral. But I confess that, though I'm called to follow you, I often withdraw my presence and withhold my love from those around me. Father, forgive me. *I confess that I am not my own, but belong to you.*

Jesus, with all your strength, you sought to offer goodness to the world and glory to your Father. But I confess that I often withhold good from others and only seek to glorify myself. Father, forgive me. *I confess that I am not my own, but belong to you.*

Silently reflect on the ways you have strayed from God's gracious authority. Confess aloud and receive God's free grace through Jesus.

Assurance

An invitation to receive the assurance of a new identity in the finished work of Christ.

Lord, even though I have sinned against you, still you have loved me and given yourself for me. My old self went to the cross with Christ. And now it is no longer I who live, but Christ who lives in and through me. I am no longer my own, but I have been bought with an unspeakable price—your very blood. Your Spirit lives in me and leads me to lay aside my weak desires for the deeper delight of living for your glory. I have been made for you, I have been bought by you, and now I belong to you. *Thanks be to God!*

Scripture Reading

The surrender to God's good and authoritative Word.

If you see in a province the oppression of the poor and the violation of justice and righteousness, do not be amazed at the matter, for the high official is watched by a higher, and there are yet higher ones over them. But this is gain for a land in every way: a king committed to cultivated fields.

He who loves money will not be satisfied with money, nor he who loves wealth with his income; this also is vanity. When goods increase, they increase who eat them, and what advantage has their owner but to see them with his eyes? Sweet is the sleep of a laborer, whether he eats little or much, but the full stomach of the rich will not let him sleep.

There is a grievous evil that I have seen under the sun: riches were kept by their owner to his hurt, and those riches were lost in a bad venture. And he is father of a son, but he has nothing in his hand. As he came from his mother's womb he shall go again, naked as he came, and shall take nothing for his toil that he may carry away in his hand. This also is a grievous evil: just as he came, so shall he go, and what gain is there to him who toils for the wind? Moreover, all his days he eats in darkness in much vexation and sickness and anger.

Behold, what I have seen to be good and fitting is to eat and drink and find enjoyment in all the toil with which one toils under the sun the few days of his life that God has given him, for this is his lot. Everyone also to whom God has given wealth and possessions and power to enjoy them, and to accept his lot and rejoice in his toil—this is the gift of God. For he will not much remember the days of his life because God keeps him occupied with joy in his heart.

Ecclesiastes 5:8-20

Prayer

An invitation to bring the needs of our bodies, hearts, and minds to the care of God.

Offer prayers for yourself and for others.

Benediction

A blessing from the authority of Scripture spoken over the people of God.
The following is based on 2 Thessalonians 2:16-17.

Now may the Lord Jesus Christ himself, and God the Father, who loved me and gave me eternal comfort and good hope through grace, comfort my heart and establish it in every good work and word. *Send me now into the world as a steward of your good gifts.*

••••○

Stewards of God

Call to Worship

An invitation from God to all humanity to behold and join the story, work, and eternal worship of Jesus. This prayer is based on John 1.

Jesus, you are the Word of God. In the beginning, you were with God, and you were God. All things were made through you; nothing was made without you. You are life, and you bring light to our dark hearts. You took on flesh and dwelt among us so we might finally see and know the Father. Open my eyes to behold your glory, glory as of the only Son from the Father, full of grace and truth. *Amen.*

Psalm 33:13-22

The LORD looks down from heaven;
he sees all the children of man;
from where he sits enthroned he looks out
on all the inhabitants of the earth,
he who fashions the hearts of them all
and observes all their deeds.
The king is not saved by his great army;
a warrior is not delivered by his great strength.
The war horse is a false hope for salvation,
and by its great might it cannot rescue.

Behold, the eye of the LORD is on those who fear him,
on those who hope in his steadfast love,
that he may deliver their soul from death
and keep them alive in famine.

Our soul waits for the LORD;
he is our help and our shield.
For our heart is glad in him,
because we trust in his holy name.
Let your steadfast love, O LORD, be upon us,
even as we hope in you.

Confession

A call to acknowledge and forsake sin against God and one another.

God of all grace, you have given me your Spirit and commissioned me as the aroma of Christ on earth. But I confess that I have taken your presence for granted and sought to satisfy my own cravings before looking to the needs of others. *Father, my heart is prone to wander.*

•••••

You have created me for relationship, but I have pulled away from my neighbors. I have lived like an island and pretended to be self-sufficient. I have believed the lie that it is more blessed to receive than to give. *Father, my heart is prone to wander.*

Silently reflect on the ways you have strayed from God's gracious authority. Confess aloud and receive God's free grace through Jesus.

Assurance

An invitation to receive the assurance of a new identity in the finished work of Christ.

While I was still a sinner, you died for me. Jesus, you were resurrected so I could know true and abundant life. While I have loved imperfectly, you have loved perfectly. While I have withheld myself from God and others, you have given yourself fully to the world. Lord, you intercede for me today, and you promise not to leave me as I am. Even now, you are at work to form me into your image, from one degree of glory to the next. You have not finished what you began in me, and you will not give up until it is done. *Thanks be to God!*

Scripture Reading

The surrender to God's good and authoritative Word.

There is an evil that I have seen under the sun, and it lies heavy on mankind: a man to whom God gives wealth, possessions, and honor, so that he lacks nothing of all that he desires, yet God does not give him power to enjoy them, but a stranger enjoys them. This is vanity; it is a grievous evil. If a man fathers a hundred children and lives many years, so that the days of his years are many, but his soul is not satisfied with life's good things, and he also has no burial, I say that a stillborn child is better off than he. For it comes in vanity and goes in darkness, and in darkness its name is covered. Moreover, it has not seen the sun or known anything, yet it finds rest rather than he. Even though he should live a thousand years twice over, yet enjoy no good—do not all go to the one place?

All the toil of man is for his mouth, yet his appetite is not satisfied. For what advantage has the wise man over the fool? And what does the poor man have who knows how to conduct himself before the living? Better is the sight of the eyes than the wandering of the appetite: this also is vanity and a striving after wind.

Whatever has come to be has already been named, and it is known what man is, and that he is not able to dispute with one stronger than he. The more words, the more vanity, and what is the advantage to man? For who knows what is good for man while he lives the few days of his vain life, which he passes like a shadow? For who can tell man what will be after him under the sun?

Ecclesiastes 6:1-12

•••••

Prayer

An invitation to bring the needs of our bodies, hearts, and minds to the care of God.

Offer prayers for yourself and for others.

Benediction

A blessing from the authority of Scripture spoken over the people of God. The following is based on 2 Corinthians 13:14.

May the grace of the Lord Jesus, the love of God the Father, and the fellowship of the Holy Spirit go with me today. *Send me now into the world as a steward of your good gifts.*

•••••

Session 2

———

What Does It Mean
To Be a Steward?

Session 2

What Does It Mean To Be a Steward?

———

Call to Worship

Jesus, you are a merciful and faithful high priest, crowned with glory and honor. You took our punishment, in our place, and graciously tasted death for us. You brought many sons and daughters to glory through suffering. Through death, you destroyed the one who has the power of death. Who are we that you are mindful of us and that you care for us? In this moment, give us confidence to draw near to your throne of grace, that we might receive the mercy and help we so desperately need. *Amen.*

Bible Conversation

Have someone read the following Scripture and discussion question out loud. Spend up to 5 minutes in discussion.

I appeal to you therefore, brothers, by the mercies of God, to present your bodies as a living sacrifice, holy and acceptable to God, which is your spiritual worship. Do not be conformed to this world, but be transformed by the renewal of your mind, that by testing you may discern what is the will of God, what is good and acceptable and perfect. **Romans 12:1-2**

▶ *What do you think it means to offer your body as a "living sacrifice"? How might approaching life in this way lead to flourishing?*

Training Notes

Watch the video entitled "What Does It Mean To Be a Steward?" found at *frontlinechurch.com/formation*. Use the notes below and fill in the blanks to follow along with the video.

We have fallen heirs to the most glorious heritage a people ever received, and each one must do his part if we wish to show that the nation is worthy of its good fortune. **Theodore Roosevelt**

Stewards of Our _____

Or do you not know that your body is a temple of the Holy Spirit within you, whom you have from God? You are not your own, for you were bought with a price. So glorify God in your body. **1 Corinthians 6:19-20**

———

[My body] governs how I interact with others and how they interact with me. I experience the world around me through it. I live with my body and do everything with it. My human life is, most obviously and simply, life in the body... We do not just have bodies; we are bodies. They are not just what we are as people but an essential part of who we are.
John Kleinig, *Wonderfully Made: A Protestant Theology of the Body*

Our bodies are a gift from God. They have been given to us as an instrument of touch, healing, protection, and presence.

Stewards of Our _____

In the days of his flesh, Jesus offered up prayers and supplications, with loud cries and tears, to him who was able to save him from death, and he was heard because of his reverence. **Hebrews 5:7**

Each emotion is a good gift, helping us to gauge our hearts and driving us to our deeper need for Jesus.

Stewards of Our _____

Whatever we do, whatever our skills and abilities, we are called to be good stewards of those talents.

Whatever you do, work heartily, as for the Lord and not for men, knowing that from the Lord you will receive the inheritance as your reward. You are serving the Lord Christ. **Colossians 3:23-24**

Stewards of Our _____

As each has received a gift, use it to serve one another, as good stewards of God's varied grace: whoever speaks, as one who speaks oracles of God; whoever serves, as one who serves by the strength that God supplies—in order that in everything God may be glorified through Jesus Christ. **1 Peter 4:10-11**

Spiritual gifts are unique ways the Spirit shows his presence among his people.

Stewards of Our _____

Look carefully then how you walk, not as unwise but as wise, making the best use of the time, because the days are evil. **Ephesians 5:15-16**

To effectively steward our lives as a sacred trust from God, we must set aside time to step into the things to which God has called us.

Discussion

Discuss the following question.

▶ *When it comes to stewarding the self, we tend to either neglect these gifts, or indulge in them. Five areas of stewardship were listed in the training. Name one or two areas you feel an invitation to grow the most, and why. Refer to the table below for examples.*

		NEGLECT	INDULGE
AREAS OF STEWARDSHIP	BODY	I fail to consistently care for my body through regular rhythms of sleep and exercise. I tend to run to unhealthy foods and controlled substances.	I am overly concerned with my appearance. If my body isn't attractive or fit, I feel devastated. I constantly compare myself to others.
	EMOTIONS	I have a hard time recognizing and naming my emotions. Whenever I begin to feel strong emotions bubble up, I push them down and work to distract myself from them.	I tend to make decisions on my own, based on how I feel, and rarely seek counsel. If something feels right and true to me, it probably is.
	NATURAL TALENTS	I undersell the talents God has given me because I don't think I'm good enough. I rarely have time or energy to invest in my talents.	I believe that my talents come primarily from my effort. I tend to use my talents for my own benefit rather than for the good of others.
	SPIRITUAL GIFTS	I am generally unaware of my spiritual gifts and unintentional about practicing them. It is hard for me to see how I might have anything to contribute to the church.	I tend to mistake giftedness for character. I can be impatient with others who don't exercise their gifts. I avoid doing anything in the church that doesn't fall in line with my spiritual gifts.
	TIME	I tend to drift through life with little planning or forethought. I am often distracted by entertainment and technology.	I have every minute of every day planned out, but have little margin for the unexpected. I am generally unwilling to change my plans in order to serve others.

Exercise

Set aside ten minutes to pray for at least one person, using the guidelines below. A leader will take the initiative to offer a concluding prayer when they sense things are drawing to a close.

The following exercise will lead your group through listening prayer. To give you direction, have someone read the following out loud.

An important way we can offer ourselves to God and each other is through prayer. Most Christians are familiar with praying their own thoughts for others. However, one of the best ways we can serve each other is through listening prayer. In listening prayer, we do not merely pray our own thoughts, but also allow God's Spirit to prompt and guide our prayers (1 Cor 14:3–4, 29–33, 39). If listening prayer is new for you, don't worry—it's probably new for others in the room as well. *Here are eight guidelines:*

1   *Start by asking if anyone would like to receive prayer. If no one volunteers, invite someone. (Are you yourself facing something hard? Take a risk and request prayer!)*

2   *Place a chair in the middle of the room, and then ask permission to lay hands on the person. As a general rule, when laying hands on someone of the opposite gender, keep your hands above the shoulders.*

3   *Pray briefly to invite the Holy Spirit's presence to bless, speak, and act. Then quietly listen to the Lord together for at least 60 seconds.*

4   *After you have taken time to listen, if any Scriptures, pictures, thoughts, or gut impressions come to mind, share them with the person, and then pray briefly in light of what you shared.*

5   *Share tentatively and humbly. Avoid grand pronouncements or definitive language like "God is telling me..." Instead, you might say, "I have a sense..." or "I felt prompted to pray for..."*

6   *Encourage those who might be feeling reluctant to share. You might quietly ask each other, "Are you getting anything?" Pastor and author Sam Storms reminds us to "make room and time... for people to express what God has laid on their heart... [I]t's okay to fail or to miss it... [N]o one will be judged or excluded or laughed at if they don't always hit the nail on the head."*

7   *Take a moment to debrief with the person who received prayer. You might ask, "Did any of that particularly stand out to you?" or "Did any of that feel particularly meaningful or accurate?" You might then ask each other a similar question as a broader group.*

8   *Finally, as a rule, what you share should be encouraging or comforting. Avoid sharing anything negative or critical. If you feel that God has brought something corrective, sensitive, or potentially life-altering to your mind, find a time to share privately with one of your leaders and let them decide on the appropriate response. To be clear, refrain from sharing about "mates, dates, babies, or moves" or other potentially life-altering circumstances.*

Benediction

To conclude your time, pray this prayer out loud together. The following is based on 2 Corinthians 13:14.

May the grace of the Lord Jesus, the love of God the Father, and the fellowship of the Holy Spirit go with us today. *Amen.*

Daily Liturgies: Week 3

———

Stewards of Self

Stewards of Self

Call to Worship

An invitation from God to all humanity to behold and join the story, work, and eternal worship of Jesus. This prayer is based on Psalm 50.

O God, you are the Mighty One who summons the riches of the earth with a word. The world and its fullness are yours. To you belong the cattle on a thousand hills, and even the sparrows rest in your care. You need no one and lack nothing, yet you command my praise—for your glory and for my joy. When my hands are full, fill me with gratitude. When my hands are empty, satisfy me with yourself. *Amen.*

Psalm 39

TO THE CHOIRMASTER: TO JEDUTHUN. A PSALM OF DAVID.

I said, "I will guard my ways,
that I may not sin with my tongue;
I will guard my mouth with a muzzle,
so long as the wicked are in my presence."
I was mute and silent;
I held my peace to no avail,
and my distress grew worse.
My heart became hot within me.
As I mused, the fire burned;
then I spoke with my tongue:

"O LORD, make me know my end
and what is the measure of my days;
let me know how fleeting I am!
Behold, you have made my days a few handbreadths,
and my lifetime is as nothing before you.
Surely all mankind stands as a mere breath! SELAH
Surely a man goes about as a shadow!
Surely for nothing they are in turmoil;
man heaps up wealth and does not know who will gather!

"And now, O Lord, for what do I wait?
My hope is in you.
Deliver me from all my transgressions.
Do not make me the scorn of the fool!
I am mute; I do not open my mouth,
for it is you who have done it.
Remove your stroke from me;
I am spent by the hostility of your hand.
When you discipline a man

with rebukes for sin,
you consume like a moth what is dear to him;
surely all mankind is a mere breath! SELAH

"Hear my prayer, O LORD,
and give ear to my cry;
hold not your peace at my tears!
For I am a sojourner with you,
a guest, like all my fathers.
Look away from me, that I may smile again,
before I depart and am no more!"

Confession

A call to acknowledge and forsake sin against God and one another.

Jesus, you warned me, "Where your treasure is, there your heart will be also."

For all the ways I have given myself to the riches of this world—forgive me and bend my heart back to you.

For all the ways I have shut my eyes to the needs of the poor—open my hands to be generous like you.

For all the ways I have preferred your blessings over your presence—change me that I might enjoy your gifts and treasure you as Giver.

For all the ways I have looked to money as my security—save me from false refuges and help me to lean on you.

Silently reflect on the ways you have strayed from God's gracious authority. Confess aloud and receive God's free grace through Jesus.

Assurance

An invitation to receive the assurance of a new identity in the finished work of Christ.

Father, you are a generous Giver. There is no good thing that you withhold from me, for it is your good pleasure to give me the kingdom. You did not spare your own Son, but gave him up for us all. Surely you will graciously provide for my every need, both now and forever. If you are for me, who can be against me? You have given me the Spirit of adoption and called me your child. Who is there to condemn? Nothing in all creation will be able to separate me from your love. *Thanks be to God!*

_____

Scripture Reading

The surrender to God's good and authoritative Word.

A good name is better than precious ointment,
and the day of death than the day of birth.
It is better to go to the house of mourning
than to go to the house of feasting,
for this is the end of all mankind,
and the living will lay it to heart.
Sorrow is better than laughter,
for by sadness of face the heart is made glad.
The heart of the wise is in the house of mourning,
but the heart of fools is in the house of mirth.
It is better for a man to hear the rebuke of the wise
than to hear the song of fools.
For as the crackling of thorns under a pot,
so is the laughter of the fools;
this also is vanity.
Surely oppression drives the wise into madness,
and a bribe corrupts the heart.
Better is the end of a thing than its beginning,
and the patient in spirit is better than the proud in spirit.
Be not quick in your spirit to become angry,
for anger lodges in the heart of fools.
Say not, "Why were the former days better than these?"
For it is not from wisdom that you ask this.
Wisdom is good with an inheritance,
an advantage to those who see the sun.
For the protection of wisdom is like the protection of money,
and the advantage of knowledge is that wisdom preserves the life of him who has it.
Consider the work of God:
who can make straight what he has made crooked?

Ecclesiastes 7:1-13

Prayer

An invitation to bring the needs of our bodies, hearts, and minds to the care of God.

Offer prayers for yourself and for others.

___

Benediction

A blessing from the authority of Scripture spoken over the people of God.
The following is based on Philippians 4:19-20.

O my God, you will supply my every need according to your riches in glory in Christ Jesus. To you, Father, be glory forever and ever. *Send me now into the world as a steward of your good gifts.*

Stewards of Self

Call to Worship

An invitation from God to all humanity to behold and join the story, work, and eternal worship of Jesus. This prayer is based on James 1.

Father of lights, every good and perfect gift comes from you. Your generosity knows no bounds and never changes. In your grace, you gave me life by the Word of truth. Today I ask for wisdom to know how to live as a steward of your gifts—remembering that you give generously to all without reproach or reservation. *Amen.*

Psalm 43

Vindicate me, O God, and defend my cause
against an ungodly people,
from the deceitful and unjust man
deliver me!
For you are the God in whom I take refuge;
why have you rejected me?
Why do I go about mourning
because of the oppression of the enemy?

Send out your light and your truth;
let them lead me;
let them bring me to your holy hill
and to your dwelling!
Then I will go to the altar of God,
to God my exceeding joy,
and I will praise you with the lyre,
O God, my God.

Why are you cast down, O my soul,
and why are you in turmoil within me?
Hope in God; for I shall again praise him,
my salvation and my God.

Confession

A call to acknowledge and forsake sin against God and one another.

I hear your call to love you with all my heart, mind, and strength. But I confess that my love for you is diluted—made weak by lesser desires and a divided heart. *I have sought my own way, and my soul is unsatisfied.*

———

You have called me to steward your creation and fill it with blessing. But I have twisted your good gifts and turned them to my own ends. *I have sought my own way, and my soul is unsatisfied.*

Silently reflect on the ways you have strayed from God's gracious authority. Confess aloud and receive God's free grace through Jesus.

Assurance

An invitation to receive the assurance of a new identity in the finished work of Christ.

Father of lights, you richly give me all things to enjoy. In Jesus, I stand clothed in purity, washed in mercy, and adopted in love. I no longer have to leave the table of the world unsatisfied. You have spread a banquet before me filled with every good thing. Surely goodness and mercy will follow me all the days of my life, and I will find satisfaction in you. *Thanks be to God!*

Scripture Reading

The surrender to God's good and authoritative Word.

In the day of prosperity be joyful, and in the day of adversity consider: God has made the one as well as the other, so that man may not find out anything that will be after him.

In my vain life I have seen everything. There is a righteous man who perishes in his righteousness, and there is a wicked man who prolongs his life in his evildoing. Be not overly righteous, and do not make yourself too wise. Why should you destroy yourself? Be not overly wicked, neither be a fool. Why should you die before your time? It is good that you should take hold of this, and from that withhold not your hand, for the one who fears God shall come out from both of them.

Wisdom gives strength to the wise man more than ten rulers who are in a city.

Surely there is not a righteous man on earth who does good and never sins.

Do not take to heart all the things that people say, lest you hear your servant cursing you. Your heart knows that many times you yourself have cursed others.

All this I have tested by wisdom. I said, "I will be wise," but it was far from me. That which has been is far off, and deep, very deep; who can find it out?

I turned my heart to know and to search out and to seek wisdom and the scheme of things, and to know the wickedness of folly and the foolishness that is madness. And I find something more bitter than death: the woman whose heart is snares and nets, and whose hands are fetters. He who pleases God escapes her, but the

———

sinner is taken by her. Behold, this is what I found, says the Preacher, while adding one thing to another to find the scheme of things— which my soul has sought repeatedly, but I have not found. One man among a thousand I found, but a woman among all these I have not found. See, this alone I found, that God made man upright, but they have sought out many schemes.

Ecclesiastes 7:14-29

Prayer

An invitation to bring the needs of our bodies, hearts, and minds to the care of God.

Offer prayers for yourself and for others.

Benediction

A blessing from the authority of Scripture spoken over the people of God. The following is based on Ephesians 3:20-21.

Now to him who is able to do far more abundantly than all I could ask or think, according to the power at work within me—to him be glory in the Church and in Christ Jesus throughout all generations, forever and ever. *Send me now into the world as a steward of your good gifts.*

Stewards of Self

——

Call to Worship

An invitation from God to all humanity to behold and join the story, work, and eternal worship of Jesus. This prayer is based on Hebrews 2 and 4.

Jesus, you are a merciful and faithful high priest, crowned with glory and honor. You took my punishment, in my place, and graciously tasted death for me. You brought many sons and daughters to glory through suffering. Through death, you destroyed the one who has the power of death. Who am I that you are mindful of me and that you care for me? In this moment, give me confidence to draw near to your throne of grace, that I might receive the mercy and help I so desperately need. *Amen.*

Psalm 48

A SONG. A PSALM OF THE SONS OF KORAH.

Great is the LORD and greatly to be praised
in the city of our God!
His holy mountain, beautiful in elevation,
is the joy of all the earth,

Mount Zion, in the far north,
the city of the great King.
Within her citadels God
has made himself known as a fortress.

For behold, the kings assembled;
they came on together.
As soon as they saw it, they were astounded;
they were in panic; they took to flight.
Trembling took hold of them there,
anguish as of a woman in labor.
By the east wind you shattered
the ships of Tarshish.
As we have heard, so have we seen
in the city of the LORD of hosts,
in the city of our God,
which God will establish forever. SELAH

We have thought on your steadfast love, O God,
in the midst of your temple.
As your name, O God,
so your praise reaches to the ends of the earth.

• • • • ◦ ◦

Your right hand is filled with righteousness.
Let Mount Zion be glad!
Let the daughters of Judah rejoice
because of your judgments!

Walk about Zion, go around her,
number her towers,
consider well her ramparts,
go through her citadels,
that you may tell the next generation
that this is God,
our God forever and ever.
He will guide us forever.

Confession

A call to acknowledge and forsake sin against God and one another.

Jesus, you loved the unlovable. You feasted with the broken and the immoral. But I confess that, though I'm called to follow you, I often withdraw my presence and withhold my love from those around me. Father, forgive me. *I confess that I am not my own, but belong to you.*

Jesus, with all your strength, you sought to offer goodness to the world and glory to your Father. But I confess that I often withhold good from others and only seek to glorify myself. Father, forgive me. *I confess that I am not my own, but belong to you.*

Silently reflect on the ways you have strayed from God's gracious authority. Confess aloud and receive God's free grace through Jesus.

Assurance

An invitation to receive the assurance of a new identity in the finished work of Christ.

Lord, even though I have sinned against you, still you have loved me and given yourself for me. My old self went to the cross with Christ. And now it is no longer I who live, but Christ who lives in and through me. I am no longer my own, but I have been bought with an unspeakable price—your very blood. Your Spirit lives in me and leads me to lay aside my weak desires for the deeper delight of living for your glory. I have been made for you, I have been bought by you, and now I belong to you. *Thanks be to God!*

_____

Scripture Reading

The surrender to God's good and authoritative Word.

Who is like the wise?
And who knows the interpretation of a thing?
A man's wisdom makes his face shine,
and the hardness of his face is changed.

I say: Keep the king's command, because of God's oath to him. Be not hasty to go from his presence. Do not take your stand in an evil cause, for he does whatever he pleases. For the word of the king is supreme, and who may say to him, "What are you doing?" Whoever keeps a command will know no evil thing, and the wise heart will know the proper time and the just way. For there is a time and a way for everything, although man's trouble lies heavy on him. For he does not know what is to be, for who can tell him how it will be? No man has power to retain the spirit, or power over the day of death. There is no discharge from war, nor will wickedness deliver those who are given to it. All this I observed while applying my heart to all that is done under the sun, when man had power over man to his hurt.

Ecclesiastes 8:1-9

Prayer

An invitation to bring the needs of our bodies, hearts, and minds to the care of God.

Offer prayers for yourself and for others.

Benediction

A blessing from the authority of Scripture spoken over the people of God.
The following is based on 2 Thessalonians 2:16-17.

Now may the Lord Jesus Christ himself, and God the Father, who loved me and gave me eternal comfort and good hope through grace, comfort my heart and establish it in every good work and word. *Send me now into the world as a steward of your good gifts.*

Stewards of Self

―――

Call to Worship

An invitation from God to all humanity to behold and join the story, work, and eternal worship of Jesus. This prayer is based on John 1.

Jesus, you are the Word of God. In the beginning, you were with God, and you were God. All things were made through you; nothing was made without you. You are life, and you bring light to our dark hearts. You took on flesh and dwelt among us so we might finally see and know the Father. Open my eyes to behold your glory, glory as of the only Son from the Father, full of grace and truth. *Amen.*

Psalm 55:1-11

TO THE CHOIRMASTER: WITH STRINGED INSTRUMENTS. A MASKIL OF DAVID.

Give ear to my prayer, O God,
and hide not yourself from my plea for mercy!
Attend to me, and answer me;
I am restless in my complaint and I moan,
because of the noise of the enemy,
because of the oppression of the wicked.
For they drop trouble upon me,
and in anger they bear a grudge against me.

My heart is in anguish within me;
the terrors of death have fallen upon me.
Fear and trembling come upon me,
and horror overwhelms me.
And I say, "Oh, that I had wings like a dove!
I would fly away and be at rest;
yes, I would wander far away;
I would lodge in the wilderness; SELAH
I would hurry to find a shelter
from the raging wind and tempest."

Destroy, O Lord, divide their tongues;
for I see violence and strife in the city.
Day and night they go around it
on its walls,
and iniquity and trouble are within it;
ruin is in its midst;
oppression and fraud
do not depart from its marketplace.

•••••

Confession

A call to acknowledge and forsake sin against God and one another.

God of all grace, you have given me your Spirit and commissioned me as the aroma of Christ on earth. But I confess that I have taken your presence for granted and sought to satisfy my own cravings before looking to the needs of others. *Father, my heart is prone to wander.*

You have created me for relationship, but I have pulled away from my neighbors. I have lived like an island and pretended to be self-sufficient. I have believed the lie that it is more blessed to receive than to give. *Father, my heart is prone to wander.*

Silently reflect on the ways you have strayed from God's gracious authority. Confess aloud and receive God's free grace through Jesus.

Assurance

An invitation to receive the assurance of a new identity in the finished work of Christ.

While I was still a sinner, you died for me. Jesus, you were resurrected so I could know true and abundant life. While I have loved imperfectly, you have loved perfectly. While I have withheld myself from God and others, you have given yourself fully to the world. Lord, you intercede for me today, and you promise not to leave me as I am. Even now, you are at work to form me into your image, from one degree of glory to the next. You have not finished what you began in me, and you will not give up until it is done. *Thanks be to God!*

Scripture Reading

The surrender to God's good and authoritative Word.

Then I saw the wicked buried. They used to go in and out of the holy place and were praised in the city where they had done such things. This also is vanity. Because the sentence against an evil deed is not executed speedily, the heart of the children of man is fully set to do evil. Though a sinner does evil a hundred times and prolongs his life, yet I know that it will be well with those who fear God, because they fear before him. But it will not be well with the wicked, neither will he prolong his days like a shadow, because he does not fear before God.

There is a vanity that takes place on earth, that there are righteous people to whom it happens according to the deeds of the wicked, and there are wicked people to whom it happens according to the deeds of the righteous. I said that this also is vanity. And I commend joy, for man has nothing better under the sun but to eat and drink and be joyful, for this will go with him in his toil through the days of his life that God has given him under the sun.

———

When I applied my heart to know wisdom, and to see the business that is done on earth, how neither day nor night do one's eyes see sleep, then I saw all the work of God, that man cannot find out the work that is done under the sun. However much man may toil in seeking, he will not find it out. Even though a wise man claims to know, he cannot find it out.

Ecclesiastes 8:10-17

Prayer

An invitation to bring the needs of our bodies, hearts, and minds to the care of God.

Offer prayers for yourself and for others.

Benediction

A blessing from the authority of Scripture spoken over the people of God. The following is based on 2 Corinthians 13:14.

May the grace of the Lord Jesus, the love of God the Father, and the fellowship of the Holy Spirit go with me today. *Send me now into the world as a steward of your good gifts.*

Stewards of Self

Call to Worship

An invitation from God to all humanity to behold and join the story, work, and eternal worship of Jesus. This prayer is based on Psalm 50.

O God, you are the Mighty One who summons the riches of the earth with a word. The world and its fullness are yours. To you belong the cattle on a thousand hills, and even the sparrows rest in your care. You need no one and lack nothing, yet you command my praise—for your glory and for my joy. When my hands are full, fill me with gratitude. When my hands are empty, satisfy me with yourself. *Amen.*

Psalm 55:12-23

For it is not an enemy who taunts me—
then I could bear it;
it is not an adversary who deals insolently with me—
then I could hide from him.
But it is you, a man, my equal,
my companion, my familiar friend.
We used to take sweet counsel together;
within God's house we walked in the throng.
Let death steal over them;
let them go down to Sheol alive;
for evil is in their dwelling place and in their heart.

But I call to God,
and the LORD will save me.
Evening and morning and at noon
I utter my complaint and moan,
and he hears my voice.
He redeems my soul in safety
from the battle that I wage,
for many are arrayed against me.
God will give ear and humble them,
he who is enthroned from of old, SELAH
because they do not change
and do not fear God.

My companion stretched out his hand against his friends;
he violated his covenant.
His speech was smooth as butter,
yet war was in his heart;
his words were softer than oil,
yet they were drawn swords.

•••••

Cast your burden on the LORD,
and he will sustain you;
he will never permit
the righteous to be moved.

But you, O God, will cast them down
into the pit of destruction;
men of blood and treachery
shall not live out half their days.
But I will trust in you.

Confession

A call to acknowledge and forsake sin against God and one another.

Jesus, you warned me, "Where your treasure is, there your heart will be also."

For all the ways I have given myself to the riches of this world—forgive me and bend my heart back to you.

For all the ways I have shut my eyes to the needs of the poor—open my hands to be generous like you.

For all the ways I have preferred your blessings over your presence—change me that I might enjoy your gifts and treasure you as Giver.

For all the ways I have looked to money as my security—save me from false refuges and help me to lean on you.

Silently reflect on the ways you have strayed from God's gracious authority. Confess aloud and receive God's free grace through Jesus.

Assurance

An invitation to receive the assurance of a new identity in the finished work of Christ.

Father, you are a generous Giver. There is no good thing that you withhold from me, for it is your good pleasure to give me the kingdom. You did not spare your own Son, but gave him up for us all. Surely you will graciously provide for my every need, both now and forever. If you are for me, who can be against me? You have given me the Spirit of adoption and called me your child. Who is there to condemn? Nothing in all creation will be able to separate me from your love. *Thanks be to God!*

•••••

Scripture Reading

The surrender to God's good and authoritative Word.

But all this I laid to heart, examining it all, how the righteous and the wise and their deeds are in the hand of God. Whether it is love or hate, man does not know; both are before him. It is the same for all, since the same event happens to the righteous and the wicked, to the good and the evil, to the clean and the unclean, to him who sacrifices and him who does not sacrifice. As the good one is, so is the sinner, and he who swears is as he who shuns an oath. This is an evil in all that is done under the sun, that the same event happens to all. Also, the hearts of the children of man are full of evil, and madness is in their hearts while they live, and after that they go to the dead. But he who is joined with all the living has hope, for a living dog is better than a dead lion. For the living know that they will die, but the dead know nothing, and they have no more reward, for the memory of them is forgotten. Their love and their hate and their envy have already perished, and forever they have no more share in all that is done under the sun.

Go, eat your bread with joy, and drink your wine with a merry heart, for God has already approved what you do.

Let your garments be always white. Let not oil be lacking on your head.

Enjoy life with the wife whom you love, all the days of your vain life that he has given you under the sun, because that is your portion in life and in your toil at which you toil under the sun. Whatever your hand finds to do, do it with your might, for there is no work or thought or knowledge or wisdom in Sheol, to which you are going.

Ecclesiastes 9:1-10

Prayer

An invitation to bring the needs of our bodies, hearts, and minds to the care of God.

Offer prayers for yourself and for others.

Benediction

A blessing from the authority of Scripture spoken over the people of God. The following is based on Philippians 4:19-20.

O my God, you will supply my every need according to your riches in glory in Christ Jesus. To you, Father, be glory forever and ever. *Send me now into the world as a steward of your good gifts.*

•••••

Daily Liturgies: Week 4

———

Stewards of Self

Stewards of Self

Call to Worship

An invitation from God to all humanity to behold and join the story, work, and eternal worship of Jesus. This prayer is based on James 1.

Father of lights, every good and perfect gift comes from you. Your generosity knows no bounds and never changes. In your grace, you gave me life by the Word of truth. Today I ask for wisdom to know how to live as a steward of your gifts—remembering that you give generously to all without reproach or reservation. *Amen.*

Psalm 59

TO THE CHOIRMASTER: ACCORDING TO DO NOT DESTROY. A MIKTAM OF DAVID, WHEN SAUL SENT MEN
TO WATCH HIS HOUSE IN ORDER TO KILL HIM.

Deliver me from my enemies, O my God;
protect me from those who rise up against me;
deliver me from those who work evil,
and save me from bloodthirsty men.

For behold, they lie in wait for my life;
fierce men stir up strife against me.
For no transgression or sin of mine, O LORD,
for no fault of mine, they run and make ready.
Awake, come to meet me, and see!
You, LORD God of hosts, are God of Israel.
Rouse yourself to punish all the nations;
spare none of those who treacherously plot evil. SELAH

Each evening they come back,
howling like dogs
and prowling about the city.
There they are, bellowing with their mouths
with swords in their lips—
for "Who," they think, "will hear us?"

But you, O LORD, laugh at them;
you hold all the nations in derision.
O my Strength, I will watch for you,
for you, O God, are my fortress.
My God in his steadfast love will meet me;
God will let me look in triumph on my enemies.

●◦◦◦◦

Kill them not, lest my people forget;
make them totter by your power and bring them down,
O Lord, our shield!
For the sin of their mouths, the words of their lips,
let them be trapped in their pride.
For the cursing and lies that they utter,
consume them in wrath;
consume them till they are no more,
that they may know that God rules over Jacob
to the ends of the earth. SELAH

Each evening they come back,
howling like dogs
and prowling about the city.
They wander about for food
and growl if they do not get their fill.

But I will sing of your strength;
I will sing aloud of your steadfast love in the morning.
For you have been to me a fortress
and a refuge in the day of my distress.
O my Strength, I will sing praises to you,
for you, O God, are my fortress,
the God who shows me steadfast love.

Confession

A call to acknowledge and forsake sin against God and one another.

I hear your call to love you with all my heart, mind, and strength. But I confess that
my love for you is diluted—made weak by lesser desires and a divided heart. *I
have sought my own way, and my soul is unsatisfied.*

You have called me to steward your creation and fill it with blessing. But I have
twisted your good gifts and turned them to my own ends. *I have sought my own
way, and my soul is unsatisfied.*

**Silently reflect on the ways you have strayed from God's gracious authority.
Confess aloud and receive God's free grace through Jesus.**

Assurance

An invitation to receive the assurance of a new identity in the finished work of Christ.

Father of lights, you richly give me all things to enjoy. In Jesus, I stand clothed in
purity, washed in mercy, and adopted in love. I no longer have to leave the table of

———

the world unsatisfied. You have spread a banquet before me filled with every good thing. Surely goodness and mercy will follow me all the days of my life, and I will find satisfaction in you. *Thanks be to God!*

Scripture Reading

The surrender to God's good and authoritative Word.

Again I saw that under the sun the race is not to the swift, nor the battle to the strong, nor bread to the wise, nor riches to the intelligent, nor favor to those with knowledge, but time and chance happen to them all. For man does not know his time. Like fish that are taken in an evil net, and like birds that are caught in a snare, so the children of man are snared at an evil time, when it suddenly falls upon them.

I have also seen this example of wisdom under the sun, and it seemed great to me. There was a little city with few men in it, and a great king came against it and besieged it, building great siegeworks against it. But there was found in it a poor, wise man, and he by his wisdom delivered the city. Yet no one remembered that poor man. But I say that wisdom is better than might, though the poor man's wisdom is despised and his words are not heard.

The words of the wise heard in quiet are better than the shouting of a ruler among fools. Wisdom is better than weapons of war, but one sinner destroys much good.

Ecclesiastes 9:11-18

Prayer

An invitation to bring the needs of our bodies, hearts, and minds to the care of God.

Offer prayers for yourself and for others.

Benediction

A blessing from the authority of Scripture spoken over the people of God. The following is based on Ephesians 3:20-21.

Now to him who is able to do far more abundantly than all I could ask or think, according to the power at work within me—to him be glory in the Church and in Christ Jesus throughout all generations, forever and ever. *Send me now into the world as a steward of your good gifts.*

Stewards of Self

___

Call to Worship

An invitation from God to all humanity to behold and join the story, work, and eternal worship of Jesus. This prayer is based on Hebrews 2 and 4.

Jesus, you are a merciful and faithful high priest, crowned with glory and honor. You took my punishment, in my place, and graciously tasted death for me. You brought many sons and daughters to glory through suffering. Through death, you destroyed the one who has the power of death. Who am I that you are mindful of me and that you care for me? In this moment, give me confidence to draw near to your throne of grace, that I might receive the mercy and help I so desperately need. *Amen.*

Psalm 61

TO THE CHOIRMASTER: WITH STRINGED INSTRUMENTS. OF DAVID.

Hear my cry, O God,
listen to my prayer;
from the end of the earth I call to you
when my heart is faint.
Lead me to the rock
that is higher than I,
for you have been my refuge,
a strong tower against the enemy.

Let me dwell in your tent forever!
Let me take refuge under the shelter of your wings! SELAH
For you, O God, have heard my vows;
you have given me the heritage of those who fear your name.

Prolong the life of the king;
may his years endure to all generations!
May he be enthroned forever before God;
appoint steadfast love and faithfulness to watch over him!

So will I ever sing praises to your name,
as I perform my vows day after day.

Confession

A call to acknowledge and forsake sin against God and one another.

Jesus, you loved the unlovable. You feasted with the broken and the immoral. But I confess that, though I'm called to follow you, I often withdraw my presence and withhold my love from those around me. Father, forgive me. *I confess that I am not my own, but belong to you.*

Jesus, with all your strength, you sought to offer goodness to the world and glory to your Father. But I confess that I often withhold good from others and only seek to glorify myself. Father, forgive me. *I confess that I am not my own, but belong to you.*

Silently reflect on the ways you have strayed from God's gracious authority. Confess aloud and receive God's free grace through Jesus.

Assurance

An invitation to receive the assurance of a new identity in the finished work of Christ.

Lord, even though I have sinned against you, still you have loved me and given yourself for me. My old self went to the cross with Christ. And now it is no longer I who live, but Christ who lives in and through me. I am no longer my own, but I have been bought with an unspeakable price—your very blood. Your Spirit lives in me and leads me to lay aside my weak desires for the deeper delight of living for your glory. I have been made for you, I have been bought by you, and now I belong to you. *Thanks be to God!*

Scripture Reading

The surrender to God's good and authoritative Word.

Dead flies make the perfumer's ointment give off a stench;
so a little folly outweighs wisdom and honor.
A wise man's heart inclines him to the right,
but a fool's heart to the left.
Even when the fool walks on the road, he lacks sense,
and he says to everyone that he is a fool.
If the anger of the ruler rises against you, do not leave your place,
for calmness will lay great offenses to rest.

There is an evil that I have seen under the sun, as it were an error proceeding from the ruler: folly is set in many high places, and the rich sit in a low place. I have seen slaves on horses, and princes walking on the ground like slaves.

He who digs a pit will fall into it,
and a serpent will bite him who breaks through a wall.
He who quarries stones is hurt by them,
and he who splits logs is endangered by them.
If the iron is blunt, and one does not sharpen the edge,
he must use more strength,
but wisdom helps one to succeed.
If the serpent bites before it is charmed,
there is no advantage to the charmer.

Ecclesiastes 10:1-11

Prayer

An invitation to bring the needs of our bodies, hearts, and minds to the care of God.

Offer prayers for yourself and for others.

Benediction

A blessing from the authority of Scripture spoken over the people of God.
The following is based on 2 Thessalonians 2:16-17.

Now may the Lord Jesus Christ himself, and God the Father, who loved me and gave me eternal comfort and good hope through grace, comfort my heart and establish it in every good work and word. *Send me now into the world as a steward of your good gifts.*

Stewards of Self

Call to Worship

An invitation from God to all humanity to behold and join the story, work, and eternal worship of Jesus. This prayer is based on John 1.

Jesus, you are the Word of God. In the beginning, you were with God, and you were God. All things were made through you; nothing was made without you. You are life, and you bring light to our dark hearts. You took on flesh and dwelt among us so we might finally see and know the Father. Open my eyes to behold your glory, glory as of the only Son from the Father, full of grace and truth. *Amen.*

Psalm 69:1-18

TO THE CHOIRMASTER: ACCORDING TO THE LILIES. OF DAVID.

Save me, O God!
For the waters have come up to my neck.
I sink in deep mire,
where there is no foothold;
I have come into deep waters,
and the flood sweeps over me.
I am weary with my crying out;
my throat is parched.
My eyes grow dim
with waiting for my God.

More in number than the hairs of my head
are those who hate me without cause;
mighty are those who would destroy me,
those who attack me with lies.
What I did not steal
must I now restore?
O God, you know my folly;
the wrongs I have done are not hidden from you.

Let not those who hope in you be put to shame through me,
O Lord GOD of hosts;
let not those who seek you be brought to dishonor through me,
O God of Israel.
For it is for your sake that I have borne reproach,
that dishonor has covered my face.
I have become a stranger to my brothers,
an alien to my mother's sons.

•••••

For zeal for your house has consumed me,
and the reproaches of those who reproach you have fallen on me.
When I wept and humbled my soul with fasting,
it became my reproach.
When I made sackcloth my clothing,
I became a byword to them.
I am the talk of those who sit in the gate,
and the drunkards make songs about me.

But as for me, my prayer is to you, O LORD.
At an acceptable time, O God,
in the abundance of your steadfast love answer me in your saving faithfulness.
Deliver me
from sinking in the mire;
let me be delivered from my enemies
and from the deep waters.
Let not the flood sweep over me,
or the deep swallow me up,
or the pit close its mouth over me.

Answer me, O LORD, for your steadfast love is good;
according to your abundant mercy, turn to me.
Hide not your face from your servant,
for I am in distress; make haste to answer me.
Draw near to my soul, redeem me;
ransom me because of my enemies!

Confession

A call to acknowledge and forsake sin against God and one another.

God of all grace, you have given me your Spirit and commissioned me as the aroma of Christ on earth. But I confess that I have taken your presence for granted and sought to satisfy my own cravings before looking to the needs of others. *Father, my heart is prone to wander.*

You have created me for relationship, but I have pulled away from my neighbors. I have lived like an island and pretended to be self-sufficient. I have believed the lie that it is more blessed to receive than to give. *Father, my heart is prone to wander.*

Silently reflect on the ways you have strayed from God's gracious authority. Confess aloud and receive God's free grace through Jesus.

_____

Assurance

An invitation to receive the assurance of a new identity in the finished work of Christ.

While I was still a sinner, you died for me. Jesus, you were resurrected so I could know true and abundant life. While I have loved imperfectly, you have loved perfectly. While I have withheld myself from God and others, you have given yourself fully to the world. Lord, you intercede for me today, and you promise not to leave me as I am. Even now, you are at work to form me into your image, from one degree of glory to the next. You have not finished what you began in me, and you will not give up until it is done. *Thanks be to God!*

Scripture Reading

The surrender to God's good and authoritative Word.

The words of a wise man's mouth win him favor,
but the lips of a fool consume him.
The beginning of the words of his mouth is foolishness,
and the end of his talk is evil madness.
A fool multiplies words,
though no man knows what is to be,
and who can tell him what will be after him?
The toil of a fool wearies him,
for he does not know the way to the city.

Woe to you, O land, when your king is a child,
and your princes feast in the morning!
Happy are you, O land, when your king is the son of the nobility,
and your princes feast at the proper time,
for strength, and not for drunkenness!
Through sloth the roof sinks in,
and through indolence the house leaks.
Bread is made for laughter,
and wine gladdens life,
and money answers everything.
Even in your thoughts, do not curse the king,
nor in your bedroom curse the rich,
for a bird of the air will carry your voice,
or some winged creature tell the matter.

Ecclesiastes 10:12-20

Prayer

An invitation to bring the needs of our bodies, hearts, and minds to the care of God.

Offer prayers for yourself and for others.

Benediction

A blessing from the authority of Scripture spoken over the people of God.
The following is based on 2 Corinthians 13:14.

May the grace of the Lord Jesus, the love of God the Father, and the fellowship of the Holy Spirit go with me today. *Send me now into the world as a steward of your good gifts.*

Stewards of Self

————

Call to Worship

An invitation from God to all humanity to behold and join the story, work, and eternal worship of Jesus. This prayer is based on Psalm 50.

O God, you are the Mighty One who summons the riches of the earth with a word. The world and its fullness are yours. To you belong the cattle on a thousand hills, and even the sparrows rest in your care. You need no one and lack nothing, yet you command my praise—for your glory and for my joy. When my hands are full, fill me with gratitude. When my hands are empty, satisfy me with yourself. *Amen*

Psalm 69:19-36

You know my reproach,
and my shame and my dishonor;
my foes are all known to you.
Reproaches have broken my heart,
so that I am in despair.
I looked for pity, but there was none,
and for comforters, but I found none.
They gave me poison for food,
and for my thirst they gave me sour wine to drink.

Let their own table before them become a snare;
and when they are at peace, let it become a trap.
Let their eyes be darkened, so that they cannot see,
and make their loins tremble continually.
Pour out your indignation upon them,
and let your burning anger overtake them.
May their camp be a desolation;
let no one dwell in their tents.
For they persecute him whom you have struck down,
and they recount the pain of those you have wounded.
Add to them punishment upon punishment;
may they have no acquittal from you.
Let them be blotted out of the book of the living;
let them not be enrolled among the righteous.

But I am afflicted and in pain;
let your salvation, O God, set me on high!

I will praise the name of God with a song;
I will magnify him with thanksgiving.
This will please the LORD more than an ox

•••• ·

or a bull with horns and hoofs.
When the humble see it they will be glad;
you who seek God, let your hearts revive.
For the LORD hears the needy
and does not despise his own people who are prisoners.

Let heaven and earth praise him,
the seas and everything that moves in them.
For God will save Zion
and build up the cities of Judah,
and people shall dwell there and possess it;
the offspring of his servants shall inherit it,
and those who love his name shall dwell in it.

Confession

A call to acknowledge and forsake sin against God and one another.

Jesus, you warned me, "Where your treasure is, there your heart will be also."

For all the ways I have given myself to the riches of this world—forgive me and bend my heart back to you.

For all the ways I have shut my eyes to the needs of the poor—open my hands to be generous like you.

For all the ways I have preferred your blessings over your presence—change me that I might enjoy your gifts and treasure you as Giver.

For all the ways I have looked to money as my security—save me from false refuges and help me to lean on you.

Silently reflect on the ways you have strayed from God's gracious authority. Confess aloud and receive God's free grace through Jesus.

Assurance

An invitation to receive the assurance of a new identity in the finished work of Christ.

Father, you are a generous Giver. There is no good thing that you withhold from me, for it is your good pleasure to give me the kingdom. You did not spare your own Son, but gave him up for us all. Surely you will graciously provide for my every need, both now and forever. If you are for me, who can be against me? You have given me the Spirit of adoption and called me your child. Who is there to condemn? Nothing in all creation will be able to separate me from your love. *Thanks be to God!*

•••••

Scripture Reading

The surrender to God's good and authoritative Word.

Cast your bread upon the waters,
for you will find it after many days.
Give a portion to seven, or even to eight,
for you know not what disaster may happen on earth.
If the clouds are full of rain,
they empty themselves on the earth,
and if a tree falls to the south or to the north,
in the place where the tree falls, there it will lie.
He who observes the wind will not sow,
and he who regards the clouds will not reap.

As you do not know the way the spirit comes to the bones in the womb of a woman
with child, so you do not know the work of God who makes everything.

In the morning sow your seed, and at evening withhold not your hand, for you do
not know which will prosper, this or that, or whether both alike will be good.

Light is sweet, and it is pleasant for the eyes to see the sun.

So if a person lives many years, let him rejoice in them all; but let him remember
that the days of darkness will be many. All that comes is vanity.

Rejoice, O young man, in your youth, and let your heart cheer you in the days of
your youth. Walk in the ways of your heart and the sight of your eyes. But know
that for all these things God will bring you into judgment.

Remove vexation from your heart, and put away pain from your body, for youth
and the dawn of life are vanity.

Ecclesiastes 11:1-10

Prayer

An invitation to bring the needs of our bodies, hearts, and minds to the care of God.

Offer prayers for yourself and for others.

Benediction

A blessing from the authority of Scripture spoken over the people of God.
The following is based on Philippians 4:19-20.

O my God, you will supply my every need according to your riches in glory in
Christ Jesus. To you, Father, be glory forever and ever. *Send me now into the world*
as a steward of your good gifts.

Stewards of Self

───

Call to Worship

An invitation from God to all humanity to behold and join the story, work, and eternal worship of Jesus. This prayer is based on James 1.

Father of lights, every good and perfect gift comes from you. Your generosity knows no bounds and never changes. In your grace, you gave me life by the Word of truth. Today I ask for wisdom to know how to live as a steward of your gifts— remembering that you give generously to all without reproach or reservation. Amen.

Psalm 72

OF SOLOMON.

Give the king your justice, O God,
and your righteousness to the royal son!
May he judge your people with righteousness,
and your poor with justice!
Let the mountains bear prosperity for the people,
and the hills, in righteousness!
May he defend the cause of the poor of the people,
give deliverance to the children of the needy,
and crush the oppressor!

May they fear you while the sun endures,
and as long as the moon, throughout all generations!
May he be like rain that falls on the mown grass,
like showers that water the earth!
In his days may the righteous flourish,
and peace abound, till the moon be no more!

May he have dominion from sea to sea,
and from the River to the ends of the earth!
May desert tribes bow down before him,
and his enemies lick the dust!
May the kings of Tarshish and of the coastlands
render him tribute;
may the kings of Sheba and Seba
bring gifts!
May all kings fall down before him,
all nations serve him!

•••••

For he delivers the needy when he calls,
the poor and him who has no helper.
He has pity on the weak and the needy,
and saves the lives of the needy.
From oppression and violence he redeems their life,
and precious is their blood in his sight.

Long may he live;
may gold of Sheba be given to him!
May prayer be made for him continually,
and blessings invoked for him all the day!
May there be abundance of grain in the land;
on the tops of the mountains may it wave;
may its fruit be like Lebanon;
and may people blossom in the cities
like the grass of the field!
May his name endure forever,
his fame continue as long as the sun!
May people be blessed in him,
all nations call him blessed!

Blessed be the LORD, the God of Israel,
who alone does wondrous things.
Blessed be his glorious name forever;
may the whole earth be filled with his glory!
Amen and Amen!

The prayers of David, the son of Jesse, are ended.

Confession

A call to acknowledge and forsake sin against God and one another.

I hear your call to love you with all my heart, mind, and strength. But I confess that
my love for you is diluted—made weak by lesser desires and a divided heart. *I
have sought my own way, and my soul is unsatisfied.*

You have called me to steward your creation and fill it with blessing. But I have
twisted your good gifts and turned them to my own ends. *I have sought my own
way, and my soul is unsatisfied.*

**Silently reflect on the ways you have strayed from God's gracious authority.
Confess aloud and receive God's free grace through Jesus.**

•••••

——

Assurance

An invitation to receive the assurance of a new identity in the finished work of Christ.

Father of lights, you richly give me all things to enjoy. In Jesus, I stand clothed in purity, washed in mercy, and adopted in love. I no longer have to leave the table of the world unsatisfied. You have spread a banquet before me filled with every good thing. Surely goodness and mercy will follow me all the days of my life, and I will find satisfaction in you.*Thanks be to God!*

Scripture Reading

The surrender to God's good and authoritative Word.

Remember also your Creator in the days of your youth, before the evil days come and the years draw near of which you will say, "I have no pleasure in them"; before the sun and the light and the moon and the stars are darkened and the clouds return after the rain, in the day when the keepers of the house tremble, and the strong men are bent, and the grinders cease because they are few, and those who look through the windows are dimmed, and the doors on the street are shut— when the sound of the grinding is low, and one rises up at the sound of a bird, and all the daughters of song are brought low— they are afraid also of what is high, and terrors are in the way; the almond tree blossoms, the grasshopper drags itself along, and desire fails, because man is going to his eternal home, and the mourners go about the streets— before the silver cord is snapped, or the golden bowl is broken, or the pitcher is shattered at the fountain, or the wheel broken at the cistern, and the dust returns to the earth as it was, and the spirit returns to God who gave it. Vanity of vanities, says the Preacher; all is vanity.

Besides being wise, the Preacher also taught the people knowledge, weighing and studying and arranging many proverbs with great care. The Preacher sought to find words of delight, and uprightly he wrote words of truth.

The words of the wise are like goads, and like nails firmly fixed are the collected sayings; they are given by one Shepherd. My son, beware of anything beyond these. Of making many books there is no end, and much study is a weariness of the flesh.

The end of the matter; all has been heard. Fear God and keep his commandments, for this is the whole duty of man. For God will bring every deed into judgment, with every secret thing, whether good or evil.

Ecclesiastes 12:1-14

•••••

Prayer

An invitation to bring the needs of our bodies, hearts, and minds to the care of God.

Offer prayers for yourself and for others.

Benediction

A blessing from the authority of Scripture spoken over the people of God. The following is based on Ephesians 3:20-21.

Now to him who is able to do far more abundantly than all I could ask or think, according to the power at work within me—to him be glory in the Church and in Christ Jesus throughout all generations, forever and ever. *Send me now into the world as a steward of your good gifts.*

•••••

Session 3

———

How Should We Steward
Our Presence?

Session 3

How Should We Steward Our Presence?

―――

Call to Worship

Jesus, you are the Word of God. In the beginning, you were with God, and you were God. All things were made through you; nothing was made without you. You are life, and you bring light to our dark hearts. You took on flesh and dwelt among us so we might finally see and know the Father. Open our eyes to behold your glory, glory as of the only Son from the Father, full of grace and truth. *Amen.*

Bible Conversation

Have someone read the following Scripture and discussion question out loud. Spend up to 5 minutes in discussion.

As you come to him, a living stone rejected by men but in the sight of God chosen and precious, you yourselves like living stones are being built up as a spiritual house, to be a holy priesthood, to offer spiritual sacrifices acceptable to God through Jesus Christ. **1 Peter 2:4-5**

▶ *Why do you think Christians are called to live as a "holy priesthood"? What would it look like to increasingly live out our priesthood with each other and with our neighbors?*

Training Notes

Watch the video entitled "How Should We Steward Our Presence?" found at *frontlinechurch.com/formation.* Use the notes below and fill in the blanks to follow along with the video.

...you yourselves like living stones are being built up as a spiritual house, to be a holy priesthood, to offer spiritual sacrifices acceptable to God through Jesus Christ. **1 Peter 2:5**

As followers of Jesus, we stand between God and humanity. We offer our lives to serve God, and we offer our presence to serve others.

The priest metaphor defines the missionary nature of the Church as a dual movement: the Church represents the world before God and she represents God before the world... Christians bless God on behalf of the world, and they bless the world on behalf of God. **Stefan Paas, *Pilgrims and Priests***

―――

Creating _____

> *Hurry is the great enemy of spiritual life in our day. You must ruthlessly eliminate hurry from your life.*
> **Dallas Willard, *quoted by John Ortberg in Soul Keeping***

We need appropriate amounts of work, appropriate amounts of play, and appropriate amounts of rest.

> *Remember the Sabbath day, to keep it holy. Six days you shall labor, and do all your work, but the seventh day is a Sabbath to the LORD your God. On it you shall not do any work...* **Exodus 20:8-10**

Sabbatical rest creates a life of prayerful presence instead of frenetic energy.

> *In our own contemporary context of the rat race of anxiety, the celebration of Sabbath is an act of resistance... It is resistance because it is a visible insistence that our lives are not defined by the production and consumption of commodity goods.* **Walter Brueggemann, *Sabbath as Resistance***

Paying _____

Stewarding our presence requires bringing as much of ourselves as we can to the present moment. We have to train ourselves to put our screens away and pay attention to where we are, to be present with the people right in front of us.

> *And your ears shall hear a word behind you, saying, "This is the way, walk in it," when you turn to the right or when you turn to the left.* **Isaiah 30:21**

Taking _____

> *Do not be deceived: God is not mocked, for whatever one sows, that will he also reap. For the one who sows to his own flesh will from the flesh reap corruption, but the one who sows to the Spirit will from the Spirit reap eternal life. And let us not grow weary of doing good, for in due season we will reap, if we do not give up.* **Galatians 6:7-9**

God has given us agency to have a real, lasting impact in our relationships, in our careers, and in our city. We must take responsibility for ourselves and the ways we are called by God to bring his peace and presence into every area of our lives.

Discussion

As in every age, God calls his children to stop, study what captures their attention in this world, weigh the consequences, and fight for undistracted hearts before him. As we live in a digital age, we should be regularly asking ourselves questions like:

▶ *Do my smartphone habits expose an underlying addiction to distractions?*

▶ *Do my smartphone habits reveal a compulsive desire to be seen and affirmed?*

▶ *Do my smartphone habits distract me from genuine communion with God?*

▶ *Do my smartphone habits preoccupy me with the pursuit of worldly success?*

▶ *Do my smartphone habits disengage me from the needs of the neighbors God has placed right in front of me?*

Let's be honest: our digital addictions (if we can call them that) are welcomed addictions. The key is to move from being distracted on purpose to being less and less distracted with an eternal purpose. The questions above sting, and they touch every area of life—God, spouse, family, friends, work, leisure, and self-projection. But this sting can lead us to make healthy changes. Every technology requires limits, and the smartphone is no exception. If you find the smartphone is absolutely necessary for your life and calling, put clear regulators in place.

Exercise

Set a timer for five minutes. Each person should silently read over and prayerfully consider these twelve common guardrails people have adopted for their relationship with technology. Check two or three guardrails that you would like to try to implement in your life. Consider what would serve you most as you seek to regain agency of one of your most precious and finite resources—your attention. After five minutes, whoever is willing can share a guardrail they checked, and how that guardrail might contribute to their flourishing.

☐ *Turn off all nonessential push notifications.*

☐ *Delete expired, nonessential, and time-wasting apps.*

☐ *At night, keep your phone out of the bedroom.*

☐ *Use a real alarm clock, not your phone alarm, to keep the phone out of your hands in the morning.*

- [ ] *Guard your morning disciplines and evening sleep patterns by using phone settings to mute notifications between one hour before bedtime to a time when you can reasonably expect to be finished with personal disciplines in the morning (e.g., 9 p.m. to 7 a.m.).*

- [ ] *Use self-restricting apps to help limit your smartphone functions and the amount of time you invest in various platforms.*

- [ ] *Recognize that much of what you respond to quickly can wait. Respond at a later, more convenient time.*

- [ ] *Even if you need to read emails on your smartphone, use strategic points during the day to respond to emails at a computer (e.g., thirty minutes each at 9 a.m. and 4 p.m.).*

- [ ] *Invite your spouse, your friends, and your family members to offer feedback on your phone habits (more than 70 percent of Christians surveyed said nobody else knew how much time they spent online).*

- [ ] *When eating with your family members or friends, leave your phone out of sight. (Studies have shown that any mobile device in the visual field of people gathering together can reduce empathy and relational connection.)*

- [ ] *When spending time with family members or friends, or when you are at church, leave your phone in a drawer or in your car, or simply power it off.*

- [ ] *At strategic moments in life, digitally detox your life and recalibrate your ultimate priorities. Step away from social media for frequent strategic stoppages (each morning), digital Sabbaths (one day offline each week), and digital sabbaticals (at least one week offline each year).*

Benediction

To conclude your time, pray this prayer out loud together, based on Philippians 4:19-20.

O my God, you will supply our every need according to your riches in glory in Christ Jesus. To you, Father, be glory forever and ever. *Amen*

Daily Liturgies: Week 5

———

Stewards
of Presence

Stewards of Presence

Call to Worship

An invitation from God to all humanity to behold and join the story, work, and eternal worship of Jesus. This prayer is based on Hebrews 2 and 4.

Jesus, you are a merciful and faithful high priest, crowned with glory and honor. You took my punishment, in my place, and graciously tasted death for me. You brought many sons and daughters to glory through suffering. Through death, you destroyed the one who has the power of death. Who am I that you are mindful of me and that you care for me? In this moment, give me confidence to draw near to your throne of grace, that I might receive the mercy and help I so desperately need. *Amen.*

Psalm 80

TO THE CHOIRMASTER: ACCORDING TO THE LILIES. A TESTIMONY. OF ASAPH, A PSALM.

Give ear, O Shepherd of Israel,
you who lead Joseph like a flock.
You who are enthroned upon the cherubim, shine forth.
Before Ephraim and Benjamin and Manasseh,
stir up your might
and come to save us!

Restore us, O God;
let your face shine, that we may be saved!

O LORD God of hosts,
how long will you be angry with your people's prayers?
You have fed them with the bread of tears
and given them tears to drink in full measure.
You make us an object of contention for our neighbors,
and our enemies laugh among themselves.

Restore us, O God of hosts;
let your face shine, that we may be saved!

You brought a vine out of Egypt;
you drove out the nations and planted it.
You cleared the ground for it;
it took deep root and filled the land.
The mountains were covered with its shade,
the mighty cedars with its branches.
It sent out its branches to the sea
and its shoots to the River.

Why then have you broken down its walls,
so that all who pass along the way pluck its fruit?
The boar from the forest ravages it,
and all that move in the field feed on it.

Turn again, O God of hosts!
Look down from heaven, and see;
have regard for this vine,
the stock that your right hand planted,
and for the son whom you made strong for yourself.
They have burned it with fire; they have cut it down;
may they perish at the rebuke of your face!
But let your hand be on the man of your right hand,
the son of man whom you have made strong for yourself!
Then we shall not turn back from you;
give us life, and we will call upon your name!

Restore us, O LORD God of hosts!
Let your face shine, that we may be saved!

Confession

A call to acknowledge and forsake sin against God and one another.

Jesus, you loved the unlovable. You feasted with the broken and the immoral. But I confess that, though I'm called to follow you, I often withdraw my presence and withhold my love from those around me. *Father, forgive me. I confess that I am not my own, but belong to you.*

Jesus, with all your strength, you sought to offer goodness to the world and glory to your Father. But I confess that I often withhold good from others and only seek to glorify myself. Father, forgive me. *I confess that I am not my own, but belong to you.*

Silently reflect on the ways you have strayed from God's gracious authority. Confess aloud and receive God's free grace through Jesus.

Assurance

An invitation to receive the assurance of a new identity in the finished work of Christ.

Lord, even though I have sinned against you, still you have loved me and given yourself for me. My old self went to the cross with Christ. And now it is no longer I who live, but Christ who lives in and through me. I am no longer my own, but I have been bought with an unspeakable price—your very blood. Your Spirit lives in me and leads me to lay aside my weak desires for the deeper delight of living for your glory. I have been made for you, I have been bought by you, and now I belong to you. *Thanks be to God!*

Scripture Reading

The surrender to God's good and authoritative Word.

I appeal to you therefore, brothers, by the mercies of God, to present your bodies as a living sacrifice, holy and acceptable to God, which is your spiritual worship. Do not be conformed to this world, but be transformed by the renewal of your mind, that by testing you may discern what is the will of God, what is good and acceptable and perfect.

For by the grace given to me I say to everyone among you not to think of himself more highly than he ought to think, but to think with sober judgment, each according to the measure of faith that God has assigned. For as in one body we have many members, and the members do not all have the same function, so we, though many, are one body in Christ, and individually members one of another. Having gifts that differ according to the grace given to us, let us use them: if prophecy, in proportion to our faith; if service, in our serving; the one who teaches, in his teaching; the one who exhorts, in his exhortation; the one who contributes, in generosity; the one who leads, with zeal; the one who does acts of mercy, with cheerfulness.

Romans 12:1-8

Prayer

An invitation to bring the needs of our bodies, hearts, and minds to the care of God.

Offer prayers for yourself and for others.

Benediction

A blessing from the authority of Scripture spoken over the people of God. The following is based on 2 Thessalonians 2:16-17.

Now may the Lord Jesus Christ himself, and God the Father, who loved me and gave me eternal comfort and good hope through grace, comfort my heart and establish it in every good work and word. *Send me now into the world as a steward of your good gifts.*

Stewards of Presence

Call to Worship

An invitation from God to all humanity to behold and join the story, work, and eternal worship of Jesus. This prayer is based on John 1.

Jesus, you are the Word of God. In the beginning, you were with God, and you were God. All things were made through you; nothing was made without you. You are life, and you bring light to our dark hearts. You took on flesh and dwelt among us so we might finally see and know the Father. Open my eyes to behold your glory, glory as of the only Son from the Father, full of grace and truth. *Amen.*

Psalm 85

TO THE CHOIRMASTER. A PSALM OF THE SONS OF KORAH.

LORD, you were favorable to your land;
you restored the fortunes of Jacob.
You forgave the iniquity of your people;
you covered all their sin. SELAH
You withdrew all your wrath;
you turned from your hot anger.

Restore us again, O God of our salvation,
and put away your indignation toward us!
Will you be angry with us forever?
Will you prolong your anger to all generations?
Will you not revive us again,
that your people may rejoice in you?
Show us your steadfast love, O LORD,
and grant us your salvation.

Let me hear what God the LORD will speak,
for he will speak peace to his people, to his saints;
but let them not turn back to folly.
Surely his salvation is near to those who fear him,
that glory may dwell in our land.

Steadfast love and faithfulness meet;
righteousness and peace kiss each other.
Faithfulness springs up from the ground,
and righteousness looks down from the sky.
Yes, the LORD will give what is good,
and our land will yield its increase.

Righteousness will go before him
and make his footsteps a way.

Confession

A call to acknowledge and forsake sin against God and one another.

God of all grace, you have given me your Spirit and commissioned me as the aroma of Christ on earth. But I confess that I have taken your presence for granted and sought to satisfy my own cravings before looking to the needs of others. *Father, my heart is prone to wander.*

You have created me for relationship, but I have pulled away from my neighbors. I have lived like an island and pretended to be self-sufficient. I have believed the lie that it is more blessed to receive than to give. *Father, my heart is prone to wander.*

Silently reflect on the ways you have strayed from God's gracious authority. Confess aloud and receive God's free grace through Jesus.

Assurance

An invitation to receive the assurance of a new identity in the finished work of Christ.

While I was still a sinner, you died for me. Jesus, you were resurrected so I could know true and abundant life. While I have loved imperfectly, you have loved perfectly. While I have withheld myself from God and others, you have given yourself fully to the world. Lord, you intercede for me today, and you promise not to leave me as I am. Even now, you are at work to form me into your image, from one degree of glory to the next. You have not finished what you began in me, and you will not give up until it is done. *Thanks be to God!*

Scripture Reading

The surrender to God's good and authoritative Word.

Let love be genuine. Abhor what is evil; hold fast to what is good. Love one another with brotherly affection. Outdo one another in showing honor. Do not be slothful in zeal, be fervent in spirit, serve the Lord. Rejoice in hope, be patient in tribulation, be constant in prayer. Contribute to the needs of the saints and seek to show hospitality.

Bless those who persecute you; bless and do not curse them. Rejoice with those who rejoice, weep with those who weep. Live in harmony with one another. Do not be haughty, but associate with the lowly. Never be wise in your own sight. Repay no one evil for evil, but give thought to do what is honorable in the sight of all. If possible, so far as it depends on you, live peaceably with all. Beloved, never avenge yourselves, but leave it to the wrath of God, for it is written, "Vengeance is mine, I will repay, says the Lord." To the contrary, "if your enemy is hungry, feed him; if he is thirsty, give him something to drink; for by so doing you will heap burning coals on his head." Do not be overcome by evil, but overcome evil with good.

Romans 12:9-21

Prayer

An invitation to bring the needs of our bodies, hearts, and minds to the care of God.

Offer prayers for yourself and for others.

Benediction

A blessing from the authority of Scripture spoken over the people of God. The following is based on 2 Corinthians 13:14.

May the grace of the Lord Jesus, the love of God the Father, and the fellowship of the Holy Spirit go with me today. *Send me now into the world as a steward of your good gifts.*

Stewards of Presence

─────

Call to Worship

An invitation from God to all humanity to behold and join the story, work, and eternal worship of Jesus. This prayer is based on Psalm 50.

O God, you are the Mighty One who summons the riches of the earth with a word. The world and its fullness are yours. To you belong the cattle on a thousand hills, and even the sparrows rest in your care. You need no one and lack nothing, yet you command my praise—for your glory and for my joy. When my hands are full, fill me with gratitude. When my hands are empty, satisfy me with yourself. *Amen.*

Psalm 86

A PRAYER OF DAVID.

Incline your ear, O LORD, and answer me,
for I am poor and needy.
Preserve my life, for I am godly;
save your servant, who trusts in you—you are my God.
Be gracious to me, O Lord,
for to you do I cry all the day.
Gladden the soul of your servant,
for to you, O Lord, do I lift up my soul.
For you, O Lord, are good and forgiving,
abounding in steadfast love to all who call upon you.
Give ear, O LORD, to my prayer;
listen to my plea for grace.
In the day of my trouble I call upon you,
for you answer me.

There is none like you among the gods, O Lord,
nor are there any works like yours.
All the nations you have made shall come
and worship before you, O Lord,
and shall glorify your name.
For you are great and do wondrous things;
you alone are God.
Teach me your way, O LORD,
that I may walk in your truth;
unite my heart to fear your name.
I give thanks to you, O Lord my God, with my whole heart,
and I will glorify your name forever.
For great is your steadfast love toward me;
you have delivered my soul from the depths of Sheol.

•••••

O God, insolent men have risen up against me;
a band of ruthless men seeks my life,
and they do not set you before them.
But you, O Lord, are a God merciful and gracious,
slow to anger and abounding in steadfast love and faithfulness.
Turn to me and be gracious to me;
give your strength to your servant,
and save the son of your maidservant.
Show me a sign of your favor,
that those who hate me may see and be put to shame
because you, LORD, have helped me and comforted me.

Confession

A call to acknowledge and forsake sin against God and one another.

Jesus, you warned me, "Where your treasure is, there your heart will be also."

For all the ways I have given myself to the riches of this world—forgive me and bend my heart back to you.

For all the ways I have shut my eyes to the needs of the poor—open my hands to be generous like you.

For all the ways I have preferred your blessings over your presence—change me that I might enjoy your gifts and treasure you as Giver.

For all the ways I have looked to money as my security—save me from false refuges and help me to lean on you.

Silently reflect on the ways you have strayed from God's gracious authority. Confess aloud and receive God's free grace through Jesus.

Assurance

An invitation to receive the assurance of a new identity in the finished work of Christ.

Father, you are a generous Giver. There is no good thing that you withhold from me, for it is your good pleasure to give me the kingdom. You did not spare your own Son, but gave him up for us all. Surely you will graciously provide for my every need, both now and forever. If you are for me, who can be against me? You have given me the Spirit of adoption and called me your child. Who is there to condemn? Nothing in all creation will be able to separate me from your love. *Thanks be to God!*

Scripture Reading

The surrender to God's good and authoritative Word.

Paul and Timothy, servants of Christ Jesus,

To all the saints in Christ Jesus who are at Philippi, with the overseers and deacons:

Grace to you and peace from God our Father and the Lord Jesus Christ.

I thank my God in all my remembrance of you, always in every prayer of mine for you all making my prayer with joy, because of your partnership in the gospel from the first day until now. And I am sure of this, that he who began a good work in you will bring it to completion at the day of Jesus Christ. It is right for me to feel this way about you all, because I hold you in my heart, for you are all partakers with me of grace, both in my imprisonment and in the defense and confirmation of the gospel. For God is my witness, how I yearn for you all with the affection of Christ Jesus. And it is my prayer that your love may abound more and more, with knowledge and all discernment, so that you may approve what is excellent, and so be pure and blameless for the day of Christ, filled with the fruit of righteousness that comes through Jesus Christ, to the glory and praise of God.

I want you to know, brothers, that what has happened to me has really served to advance the gospel, so that it has become known throughout the whole imperial guard and to all the rest that my imprisonment is for Christ. And most of the brothers, having become confident in the Lord by my imprisonment, are much more bold to speak the word without fear.

Some indeed preach Christ from envy and rivalry, but others from good will. The latter do it out of love, knowing that I am put here for the defense of the gospel. The former proclaim Christ out of selfish ambition, not sincerely but thinking to afflict me in my imprisonment. What then? Only that in every way, whether in pretense or in truth, Christ is proclaimed, and in that I rejoice.

Philippians 1:1-18

Prayer

An invitation to bring the needs of our bodies, hearts, and minds to the care of God.

Offer prayers for yourself and for others.

Benediction

A blessing from the authority of Scripture spoken over the people of God. The following is based on Philippians 4:19-20.

O my God, you will supply my every need according to your riches in glory in Christ Jesus. To you, Father, be glory forever and ever. *Send me now into the world as a steward of your good gifts.*

Stewards of Presence

____

Call to Worship

An invitation from God to all humanity to behold and join the story, work, and eternal worship of Jesus. This prayer is based on James 1.

Father of lights, every good and perfect gift comes from you. Your generosity knows no bounds and never changes. In your grace, you gave me life by the Word of truth. Today I ask for wisdom to know how to live as a steward of your gifts—remembering that you give generously to all without reproach or reservation. *Amen.*

Psalm 91

He who dwells in the shelter of the Most High
will abide in the shadow of the Almighty.
I will say to the LORD, "My refuge and my fortress,
my God, in whom I trust."

For he will deliver you from the snare of the fowler
and from the deadly pestilence.
He will cover you with his pinions,
and under his wings you will find refuge;
his faithfulness is a shield and buckler.
You will not fear the terror of the night,
nor the arrow that flies by day,
nor the pestilence that stalks in darkness,
nor the destruction that wastes at noonday.

A thousand may fall at your side,
ten thousand at your right hand,
but it will not come near you.
You will only look with your eyes
and see the recompense of the wicked.

Because you have made the LORD your dwelling place—
the Most High, who is my refuge—
no evil shall be allowed to befall you,
no plague come near your tent.

For he will command his angels concerning you
to guard you in all your ways.
On their hands they will bear you up,
lest you strike your foot against a stone.
You will tread on the lion and the adder;
the young lion and the serpent you will trample underfoot.

"Because he holds fast to me in love, I will deliver him;
I will protect him, because he knows my name.
When he calls to me, I will answer him;
I will be with him in trouble;
I will rescue him and honor him.
With long life I will satisfy him
and show him my salvation."

Confession

A call to acknowledge and forsake sin against God and one another.

I hear your call to love you with all my heart, mind, and strength. But I confess that my love for you is diluted—made weak by lesser desires and a divided heart. I have sought my own way, and my soul is unsatisfied.

You have called me to steward your creation and fill it with blessing. But I have twisted your good gifts and turned them to my own ends. I have sought my own way, and my soul is unsatisfied.

Silently reflect on the ways you have strayed from God's gracious authority. Confess aloud and receive God's free grace through Jesus.

Assurance

An invitation to receive the assurance of a new identity in the finished work of Christ.

Father of lights, you richly give me all things to enjoy. In Jesus, I stand clothed in purity, washed in mercy, and adopted in love. I no longer have to leave the table of the world unsatisfied. You have spread a banquet before me filled with every good thing. Surely goodness and mercy will follow me all the days of my life, and I will find satisfaction in you. *Thanks be to God!*

Scripture Reading

The surrender to God's good and authoritative Word.

Yes, and I will rejoice, for I know that through your prayers and the help of the Spirit of Jesus Christ this will turn out for my deliverance, as it is my eager expectation and hope that I will not be at all ashamed, but that with full courage now as always Christ will be honored in my body, whether by life or by death. For to me to live is Christ, and to die is gain. If I am to live in the flesh, that means fruitful labor for me. Yet which I shall choose I cannot tell. I am hard pressed between the two. My desire is to depart and be with Christ, for that is far better. But to remain in the flesh is more necessary on your account. Convinced of this, I know that I will remain and continue with you all, for your progress and joy in the faith, so that in me you may have ample cause to glory in Christ Jesus, because of my coming to you again.

Only let your manner of life be worthy of the gospel of Christ, so that whether I come and see you or am absent, I may hear of you that you are standing firm in one spirit, with one mind striving side by side for the faith of the gospel, and not frightened in anything by your opponents. This is a clear sign to them of their destruction, but of your salvation, and that from God. For it has been granted to you that for the sake of Christ you should not only believe in him but also suffer for his sake, engaged in the same conflict that you saw I had and now hear that I still have.

Philippians 1:18-30

Prayer

An invitation to bring the needs of our bodies, hearts, and minds to the care of God.

Offer prayers for yourself and for others.

Benediction

A blessing from the authority of Scripture spoken over the people of God.
The following is based on Ephesians 3:20-21.

Now to him who is able to do far more abundantly than all I could ask or think, according to the power at work within me—to him be glory in the Church and in Christ Jesus throughout all generations, forever and ever. *Send me now into the world as a steward of your good gifts.*

•••••◦

Stewards of Presence

———

Call to Worship

An invitation from God to all humanity to behold and join the story, work, and eternal worship of Jesus. This prayer is based on Hebrews 2 and 4.

Jesus, you are a merciful and faithful high priest, crowned with glory and honor. You took my punishment, in my place, and graciously tasted death for me. You brought many sons and daughters to glory through suffering. Through death, you destroyed the one who has the power of death. Who am I that you are mindful of me and that you care for me? In this moment, give me confidence to draw near to your throne of grace, that I might receive the mercy and help I so desperately need. *Amen.*

Psalm 100

A PSALM FOR GIVING THANKS.

Make a joyful noise to the LORD, all the earth!
Serve the LORD with gladness!
Come into his presence with singing!

Know that the LORD, he is God!
It is he who made us, and we are his;
we are his people, and the sheep of his pasture.

Enter his gates with thanksgiving,
and his courts with praise!
Give thanks to him; bless his name!

For the LORD is good;
his steadfast love endures forever,
and his faithfulness to all generations.

Confession

A call to acknowledge and forsake sin against God and one another.

Jesus, you loved the unlovable. You feasted with the broken and the immoral. But I confess that, though I'm called to follow you, I often withdraw my presence and withhold my love from those around me. Father, forgive me. *I confess that I am not my own, but belong to you.*

•••••

Jesus, with all your strength, you sought to offer goodness to the world and glory to your Father. But I confess that I often withhold good from others and only seek to glorify myself. Father, forgive me. *I confess that I am not my own, but belong to you.*

Silently reflect on the ways you have strayed from God's gracious authority. Confess aloud and receive God's free grace through Jesus.

Assurance

An invitation to receive the assurance of a new identity in the finished work of Christ.

Lord, even though I have sinned against you, still you have loved me and given yourself for me. My old self went to the cross with Christ. And now it is no longer I who live, but Christ who lives in and through me. I am no longer my own, but I have been bought with an unspeakable price—your very blood. Your Spirit lives in me and leads me to lay aside my weak desires for the deeper delight of living for your glory. I have been made for you, I have been bought by you, and now I belong to you. *Thanks be to God!*

Scripture Reading

The surrender to God's good and authoritative Word.

So if there is any encouragement in Christ, any comfort from love, any participation in the Spirit, any affection and sympathy, complete my joy by being of the same mind, having the same love, being in full accord and of one mind. Do nothing from selfish ambition or conceit, but in humility count others more significant than yourselves. Let each of you look not only to his own interests, but also to the interests of others. Have this mind among yourselves, which is yours in Christ Jesus, who, though he was in the form of God, did not count equality with God a thing to be grasped, but emptied himself, by taking the form of a servant, being born in the likeness of men. And being found in human form, he humbled himself by becoming obedient to the point of death, even death on a cross. Therefore God has highly exalted him and bestowed on him the name that is above every name, so that at the name of Jesus every knee should bow, in heaven and on earth and under the earth, and every tongue confess that Jesus Christ is Lord, to the glory of God the Father.

Therefore, my beloved, as you have always obeyed, so now, not only as in my presence but much more in my absence, work out your own salvation with fear and trembling, for it is God who works in you, both to will and to work for his good pleasure.

Philippians 2:1-13

_____

Prayer

An invitation to bring the needs of our bodies, hearts, and minds to the care of God.

Offer prayers for yourself and for others.

Benediction

A blessing from the authority of Scripture spoken over the people of God.
The following is based on 2 Thessalonians 2:16-17.

Now may the Lord Jesus Christ himself, and God the Father, who loved me and gave me eternal comfort and good hope through grace, comfort my heart and establish it in every good work and word. *Send me now into the world as a steward of your good gifts.*

Daily Liturgies: Week 6

———

Stewards
of Presence

Stewards of Presence

——

Call to Worship

An invitation from God to all humanity to behold and join the story, work, and eternal worship of Jesus. This prayer is based on John 1.

Jesus, you are the Word of God. In the beginning, you were with God, and you were God. All things were made through you; nothing was made without you. You are life, and you bring light to our dark hearts. You took on flesh and dwelt among us so we might finally see and know the Father. Open my eyes to behold your glory, glory as of the only Son from the Father, full of grace and truth. Amen.

Psalm 104:1-15

Bless the LORD, O my soul!
O LORD my God, you are very great!
You are clothed with splendor and majesty,
covering yourself with light as with a garment,
stretching out the heavens like a tent.
He lays the beams of his chambers on the waters;
he makes the clouds his chariot;
he rides on the wings of the wind;
he makes his messengers winds,
his ministers a flaming fire.

He set the earth on its foundations,
so that it should never be moved.
You covered it with the deep as with a garment;
the waters stood above the mountains.
At your rebuke they fled;
at the sound of your thunder they took to flight.
The mountains rose, the valleys sank down
to the place that you appointed for them.
You set a boundary that they may not pass,
so that they might not again cover the earth.

You make springs gush forth in the valleys;
they flow between the hills;
they give drink to every beast of the field;
the wild donkeys quench their thirst.
Beside them the birds of the heavens dwell;
they sing among the branches.
From your lofty abode you water the mountains;
the earth is satisfied with the fruit of your work.

You cause the grass to grow for the livestock
and plants for man to cultivate,
that he may bring forth food from the earth
and wine to gladden the heart of man,
oil to make his face shine
and bread to strengthen man's heart.

Confession

A call to acknowledge and forsake sin against God and one another.

God of all grace, you have given me your Spirit and commissioned me as the aroma of Christ on earth. But I confess that I have taken your presence for granted and sought to satisfy my own cravings before looking to the needs of others. *Father, my heart is prone to wander.*

You have created me for relationship, but I have pulled away from my neighbors. I have lived like an island and pretended to be self-sufficient. I have believed the lie that it is more blessed to receive than to give. *Father, my heart is prone to wander.*

Silently reflect on the ways you have strayed from God's gracious authority. Confess aloud and receive God's free grace through Jesus.

Assurance

An invitation to receive the assurance of a new identity in the finished work of Christ.

While I was still a sinner, you died for me. Jesus, you were resurrected so I could know true and abundant life. While I have loved imperfectly, you have loved perfectly. While I have withheld myself from God and others, you have given yourself fully to the world. Lord, you intercede for me today, and you promise not to leave me as I am. Even now, you are at work to form me into your image, from one degree of glory to the next. You have not finished what you began in me, and you will not give up until it is done. *Thanks be to God!*

Scripture Reading

The surrender to God's good and authoritative Word.

Do all things without grumbling or disputing, that you may be blameless and innocent, children of God without blemish in the midst of a crooked and twisted generation, among whom you shine as lights in the world, holding fast to the word of life, so that in the day of Christ I may be proud that I did not run in vain or labor in vain. Even if I am to be poured out as a drink offering upon the sacrificial offering of your faith, I am glad and rejoice with you all. Likewise you also should be glad and rejoice with me.

I hope in the Lord Jesus to send Timothy to you soon, so that I too may be cheered by news of you. For I have no one like him, who will be genuinely concerned for your welfare. For they all seek their own interests, not those of Jesus Christ. But you know Timothy's proven worth, how as a son with a father he has served with me in the gospel. I hope therefore to send him just as soon as I see how it will go with me, and I trust in the Lord that shortly I myself will come also.

I have thought it necessary to send to you Epaphroditus my brother and fellow worker and fellow soldier, and your messenger and minister to my need, for he has been longing for you all and has been distressed because you heard that he was ill. Indeed he was ill, near to death. But God had mercy on him, and not only on him but on me also, lest I should have sorrow upon sorrow. I am the more eager to send him, therefore, that you may rejoice at seeing him again, and that I may be less anxious. So receive him in the Lord with all joy, and honor such men, for he nearly died for the work of Christ, risking his life to complete what was lacking in your service to me.

Philippians 2:14-30

Prayer

An invitation to bring the needs of our bodies, hearts, and minds to the care of God.

Offer prayers for yourself and for others.

Benediction

A blessing from the authority of Scripture spoken over the people of God.
The following is based on 2 Corinthians 13:14.

May the grace of the Lord Jesus, the love of God the Father, and the fellowship of the Holy Spirit go with me today. *Send me now into the world as a steward of your good gifts.*

Stewards of Presence

Call to Worship

An invitation from God to all humanity to behold and join the story, work, and eternal worship of Jesus. This prayer is based on Psalm 50.

O God, you are the Mighty One who summons the riches of the earth with a word. The world and its fullness are yours. To you belong the cattle on a thousand hills, and even the sparrows rest in your care. You need no one and lack nothing, yet you command my praise—for your glory and for my joy. When my hands are full, fill me with gratitude. When my hands are empty, satisfy me with yourself. Amen.

Psalm 104:16-35

The trees of the LORD are watered abundantly,
the cedars of Lebanon that he planted.
In them the birds build their nests;
the stork has her home in the fir trees.
The high mountains are for the wild goats;
the rocks are a refuge for the rock badgers.

He made the moon to mark the seasons;
the sun knows its time for setting.
You make darkness, and it is night,
when all the beasts of the forest creep about.
The young lions roar for their prey,
seeking their food from God.
When the sun rises, they steal away
and lie down in their dens.
Man goes out to his work
and to his labor until the evening.

O LORD, how manifold are your works!
In wisdom have you made them all;
the earth is full of your creatures.
Here is the sea, great and wide,
which teems with creatures innumerable,
living things both small and great.
There go the ships,
and Leviathan, which you formed to play in it.

These all look to you,
to give them their food in due season.
When you give it to them, they gather it up;
when you open your hand, they are filled with good things.

When you hide your face, they are dismayed;
when you take away their breath, they die
and return to their dust.
When you send forth your Spirit, they are created,
and you renew the face of the ground.

May the glory of the LORD endure forever;
may the LORD rejoice in his works,
who looks on the earth and it trembles,
who touches the mountains and they smoke!
I will sing to the LORD as long as I live;
I will sing praise to my God while I have being.
May my meditation be pleasing to him,
for I rejoice in the LORD.
Let sinners be consumed from the earth,
and let the wicked be no more!
Bless the LORD, O my soul!
Praise the LORD!

Confession

A call to acknowledge and forsake sin against God and one another.

Jesus, you warned me, "Where your treasure is, there your heart will be also."

For all the ways I have given myself to the riches of this world—forgive me and bend my heart back to you.

For all the ways I have shut my eyes to the needs of the poor—open my hands to be generous like you.

For all the ways I have preferred your blessings over your presence—change me that I might enjoy your gifts and treasure you as Giver.

For all the ways I have looked to money as my security—save me from false refuges and help me to lean on you.

Silently reflect on the ways you have strayed from God's gracious authority. Confess aloud and receive God's free grace through Jesus.

Assurance

An invitation to receive the assurance of a new identity in the finished work of Christ.

Father, you are a generous Giver. There is no good thing that you withhold from me, for it is your good pleasure to give me the kingdom. You did not spare your own Son, but gave him up for us all. Surely you will graciously provide for my every need, both now and forever. If you are for me, who can be against me? You have given me the Spirit of adoption and called me your child. Who is there to condemn? Nothing in all creation will be able to separate me from your love. *Thanks be to God!*

Scripture Reading

The surrender to God's good and authoritative Word.

Finally, my brothers, rejoice in the Lord. To write the same things to you is no trouble to me and is safe for you.

Look out for the dogs, look out for the evildoers, look out for those who mutilate the flesh. For we are the circumcision, who worship by the Spirit of God and glory in Christ Jesus and put no confidence in the flesh— though I myself have reason for confidence in the flesh also. If anyone else thinks he has reason for confidence in the flesh, I have more: circumcised on the eighth day, of the people of Israel, of the tribe of Benjamin, a Hebrew of Hebrews; as to the law, a Pharisee; as to zeal, a persecutor of the church; as to righteousness under the law, blameless. But whatever gain I had, I counted as loss for the sake of Christ. Indeed, I count everything as loss because of the surpassing worth of knowing Christ Jesus my Lord. For his sake I have suffered the loss of all things and count them as rubbish, in order that I may gain Christ and be found in him, not having a righteousness of my own that comes from the law, but that which comes through faith in Christ, the righteousness from God that depends on faith— that I may know him and the power of his resurrection, and may share his sufferings, becoming like him in his death, that by any means possible I may attain the resurrection from the dead.

Philippians 3:1-11

Prayer

An invitation to bring the needs of our bodies, hearts, and minds to the care of God.

Offer prayers for yourself and for others.

Benediction

A blessing from the authority of Scripture spoken over the people of God. The following is based on Philippians 4:19-20.

O my God, you will supply my every need according to your riches in glory in Christ Jesus. To you, Father, be glory forever and ever. *Send me now into the world as a steward of your good gifts.*

Stewards of Presence

Call to Worship

An invitation from God to all humanity to behold and join the story, work, and eternal worship of Jesus. This prayer is based on James 1.

Father of lights, every good and perfect gift comes from you. Your generosity knows no bounds and never changes. In your grace, you gave me life by the Word of truth. Today I ask for wisdom to know how to live as a steward of your gifts—remembering that you give generously to all without reproach or reservation. Amen.

Psalm 106:1-15

Praise the LORD!
Oh give thanks to the LORD, for he is good,
for his steadfast love endures forever!
Who can utter the mighty deeds of the LORD,
or declare all his praise?
Blessed are they who observe justice,
who do righteousness at all times!

Remember me, O LORD, when you show favor to your people;
help me when you save them,
that I may look upon the prosperity of your chosen ones,
that I may rejoice in the gladness of your nation,
that I may glory with your inheritance.

Both we and our fathers have sinned;
we have committed iniquity; we have done wickedness.
Our fathers, when they were in Egypt,
did not consider your wondrous works;
they did not remember the abundance of your steadfast love,
but rebelled by the sea, at the Red Sea.
Yet he saved them for his name's sake,
that he might make known his mighty power.
He rebuked the Red Sea, and it became dry,
and he led them through the deep as through a desert.
So he saved them from the hand of the foe
and redeemed them from the power of the enemy.
And the waters covered their adversaries;
not one of them was left.
Then they believed his words;
they sang his praise.

But they soon forgot his works;
they did not wait for his counsel.
But they had a wanton craving in the wilderness,
and put God to the test in the desert;
he gave them what they asked,
but sent a wasting disease among them.

Confession

A call to acknowledge and forsake sin against God and one another.

I hear your call to love you with all my heart, mind, and strength. But I confess that my love for you is diluted—made weak by lesser desires and a divided heart. *I have sought my own way, and my soul is unsatisfied.*

You have called me to steward your creation and fill it with blessing. But I have twisted your good gifts and turned them to my own ends. *I have sought my own way, and my soul is unsatisfied.*

Silently reflect on the ways you have strayed from God's gracious authority. Confess aloud and receive God's free grace through Jesus.

Assurance

An invitation to receive the assurance of a new identity in the finished work of Christ.

Father of lights, you richly give me all things to enjoy. In Jesus, I stand clothed in purity, washed in mercy, and adopted in love. I no longer have to leave the table of the world unsatisfied. You have spread a banquet before me filled with every good thing. Surely goodness and mercy will follow me all the days of my life, and I will find satisfaction in you. *Thanks be to God!*

Scripture Reading

The surrender to God's good and authoritative Word.

Not that I have already obtained this or am already perfect, but I press on to make it my own, because Christ Jesus has made me his own. Brothers, I do not consider that I have made it my own. But one thing I do: forgetting what lies behind and straining forward to what lies ahead, I press on toward the goal for the prize of the upward call of God in Christ Jesus. Let those of us who are mature think this way, and if in anything you think otherwise, God will reveal that also to you. Only let us hold true to what we have attained.

Brothers, join in imitating me, and keep your eyes on those who walk according to the example you have in us. For many, of whom I have often told you and now tell you even with tears, walk as enemies of the cross of Christ. Their end is destruction, their god is their belly, and they glory in their shame, with minds set on earthly things. But our citizenship is in heaven, and from it we await a Savior, the Lord Jesus Christ, who will transform our lowly body to be like his glorious body, by the power that enables him even to subject all things to himself.

Philippians 3:12-21

Prayer

An invitation to bring the needs of our bodies, hearts, and minds to the care of God.

Offer prayers for yourself and for others.

Benediction

A blessing from the authority of Scripture spoken over the people of God. The following is based on Ephesians 3:20-21.

Now to him who is able to do far more abundantly than all I could ask or think, according to the power at work within me—to him be glory in the Church and in Christ Jesus throughout all generations, forever and ever. *Send me now into the world as a steward of your good gifts.*

Stewards of Presence

———

Call to Worship

An invitation from God to all humanity to behold and join the story, work, and eternal worship of Jesus. This prayer is based on Hebrews 2 and 4.

Jesus, you are a merciful and faithful high priest, crowned with glory and honor. You took my punishment, in my place, and graciously tasted death for me. You brought many sons and daughters to glory through suffering. Through death, you destroyed the one who has the power of death. Who am I that you are mindful of me and that you care for me? In this moment, give me confidence to draw near to your throne of grace, that I might receive the mercy and help I so desperately need. *Amen.*

Psalm 106:16-31

When men in the camp were jealous of Moses
and Aaron, the holy one of the LORD,
the earth opened and swallowed up Dathan,
and covered the company of Abiram.
Fire also broke out in their company;
the flame burned up the wicked.

They made a calf in Horeb
and worshiped a metal image.
They exchanged the glory of God
for the image of an ox that eats grass.
They forgot God, their Savior,
who had done great things in Egypt,
wondrous works in the land of Ham,
and awesome deeds by the Red Sea.
Therefore he said he would destroy them—
had not Moses, his chosen one,
stood in the breach before him,
to turn away his wrath from destroying them.

Then they despised the pleasant land,
having no faith in his promise.
They murmured in their tents,
and did not obey the voice of the LORD.
Therefore he raised his hand and swore to them
that he would make them fall in the wilderness,
and would make their offspring fall among the nations,
scattering them among the lands.

●●●●

Then they yoked themselves to the Baal of Peor,
and ate sacrifices offered to the dead;
they provoked the LORD to anger with their deeds,
and a plague broke out among them.
Then Phinehas stood up and intervened,
and the plague was stayed.
And that was counted to him as righteousness
from generation to generation forever.

Confession

A call to acknowledge and forsake sin against God and one another.

Jesus, you loved the unlovable. You feasted with the broken and the immoral. But I confess that, though I'm called to follow you, I often withdraw my presence and withhold my love from those around me. Father, forgive me. *I confess that I am not my own, but belong to you.*

Jesus, with all your strength, you sought to offer goodness to the world and glory to your Father. But I confess that I often withhold good from others and only seek to glorify myself. Father, forgive me. *I confess that I am not my own, but belong to you.*

Silently reflect on the ways you have strayed from God's gracious authority. Confess aloud and receive God's free grace through Jesus.

Assurance

An invitation to receive the assurance of a new identity in the finished work of Christ.

Lord, even though I have sinned against you, still you have loved me and given yourself for me. My old self went to the cross with Christ. And now it is no longer I who live, but Christ who lives in and through me. I am no longer my own, but I have been bought with an unspeakable price—your very blood. Your Spirit lives in me and leads me to lay aside my weak desires for the deeper delight of living for your glory. I have been made for you, I have been bought by you, and now I belong to you. *Thanks be to God!*

Scripture Reading

The surrender to God's good and authoritative Word.

Therefore, my brothers, whom I love and long for, my joy and crown, stand firm thus in the Lord, my beloved.

I entreat Euodia and I entreat Syntyche to agree in the Lord. Yes, I ask you also, true companion, help these women, who have labored side by side with me in the gospel together with Clement and the rest of my fellow workers, whose names are in the book of life.

Rejoice in the Lord always; again I will say, rejoice. Let your reasonableness be known to everyone. The Lord is at hand; do not be anxious about anything, but in everything by prayer and supplication with thanksgiving let your requests be made known to God. And the peace of God, which surpasses all understanding, will guard your hearts and your minds in Christ Jesus.

Finally, brothers, whatever is true, whatever is honorable, whatever is just, whatever is pure, whatever is lovely, whatever is commendable, if there is any excellence, if there is anything worthy of praise, think about these things. What you have learned and received and heard and seen in me—practice these things, and the God of peace will be with you.

Philippians 4:1-9

Prayer

An invitation to bring the needs of our bodies, hearts, and minds to the care of God.

Offer prayers for yourself and for others.

Benediction

A blessing from the authority of Scripture spoken over the people of God. The following is based on 2 Thessalonians 2:16-17.

Now may the Lord Jesus Christ himself, and God the Father, who loved me and gave me eternal comfort and good hope through grace, comfort my heart and establish it in every good work and word. *Send me now into the world as a steward of your good gifts.*

Stewards of Presence

––––

Call to Worship

An invitation from God to all humanity to behold and join the story, work, and eternal worship of Jesus. This prayer is based on John 1.

Jesus, you are the Word of God. In the beginning, you were with God, and you were God. All things were made through you; nothing was made without you. You are life, and you bring light to our dark hearts. You took on flesh and dwelt among us so we might finally see and know the Father. Open my eyes to behold your glory, glory as of the only Son from the Father, full of grace and truth. Amen.

Psalm 106:32-48

They angered him at the waters of Meribah,
and it went ill with Moses on their account,
for they made his spirit bitter,
and he spoke rashly with his lips.

They did not destroy the peoples,
as the LORD commanded them,
but they mixed with the nations
and learned to do as they did.
They served their idols,
which became a snare to them.
They sacrificed their sons
and their daughters to the demons;
they poured out innocent blood,
the blood of their sons and daughters,
whom they sacrificed to the idols of Canaan,
and the land was polluted with blood.
Thus they became unclean by their acts,
and played the whore in their deeds.

Then the anger of the LORD was kindled against his people,
and he abhorred his heritage;
he gave them into the hand of the nations,
so that those who hated them ruled over them.
Their enemies oppressed them,
and they were brought into subjection under their power.
Many times he delivered them,
but they were rebellious in their purposes
and were brought low through their iniquity.

Nevertheless, he looked upon their distress,
when he heard their cry.

•••••

For their sake he remembered his covenant,
and relented according to the abundance of his steadfast love.
He caused them to be pitied
by all those who held them captive.

Save us, O LORD our God,
and gather us from among the nations,
that we may give thanks to your holy name
and glory in your praise.

Blessed be the LORD, the God of Israel,
from everlasting to everlasting!
And let all the people say, "Amen!"
Praise the LORD!

Confession

A call to acknowledge and forsake sin against God and one another.

God of all grace, you have given me your Spirit and commissioned me as the aroma of Christ on earth. But I confess that I have taken your presence for granted and sought to satisfy my own cravings before looking to the needs of others. *Father, my heart is prone to wander.*

You have created me for relationship, but I have pulled away from my neighbors. I have lived like an island and pretended to be self-sufficient. I have believed the lie that it is more blessed to receive than to give. *Father, my heart is prone to wander.*

Silently reflect on the ways you have strayed from God's gracious authority. Confess aloud and receive God's free grace through Jesus.

Assurance

An invitation to receive the assurance of a new identity in the finished work of Christ.

While I was still a sinner, you died for me. Jesus, you were resurrected so I could know true and abundant life. While I have loved imperfectly, you have loved perfectly. While I have withheld myself from God and others, you have given yourself fully to the world. Lord, you intercede for me today, and you promise not to leave me as I am. Even now, you are at work to form me into your image, from one degree of glory to the next. You have not finished what you began in me, and you will not give up until it is done. *Thanks be to God!*

Scripture Reading

The surrender to God's good and authoritative Word.

I rejoiced in the Lord greatly that now at length you have revived your concern for me. You were indeed concerned for me, but you had no opportunity. Not that I am speaking of being in need, for I have learned in whatever situation I am to be content. I know how to be brought low, and I know how to abound. In any and every circumstance, I have learned the secret of facing plenty and hunger, abundance and need. I can do all things through him who strengthens me.

Yet it was kind of you to share my trouble. And you Philippians yourselves know that in the beginning of the gospel, when I left Macedonia, no church entered into partnership with me in giving and receiving, except you only. Even in Thessalonica you sent me help for my needs once and again. Not that I seek the gift, but I seek the fruit that increases to your credit. I have received full payment, and more. I am well supplied, having received from Epaphroditus the gifts you sent, a fragrant offering, a sacrifice acceptable and pleasing to God. And my God will supply every need of yours according to his riches in glory in Christ Jesus. To our God and Father be glory forever and ever. Amen.

Greet every saint in Christ Jesus. The brothers who are with me greet you. All the saints greet you, especially those of Caesar's household.

The grace of the Lord Jesus Christ be with your spirit.

Philippians 4:10-23

Prayer

An invitation to bring the needs of our bodies, hearts, and minds to the care of God.

Offer prayers for yourself and for others.

Benediction

A blessing from the authority of Scripture spoken over the people of God. The following is based on 2 Corinthians 13:14.

May the grace of the Lord Jesus, the love of God the Father, and the fellowship of the Holy Spirit go with me today. *Send me now into the world as a steward of your good gifts.*

———

How Should We Steward
Our Money?

How Should We Steward Our Money?

——

Call to Worship

As you begin, have someone pray this prayer out loud for the group.
This prayer is based on Psalm 50.

O God, you are the Mighty One who summons the riches of the earth with a word. The world and its fullness are yours. To you belong the cattle on a thousand hills, and even the sparrows rest in your care. You need no one and lack nothing, yet you command our praise—for your glory and for our joy. When our hands are full, fill us with gratitude. When our hands are empty, satisfy us with yourself. *Amen.*

Bible Conversation

Have someone read the following Scripture and discussion question out loud.
Spend up to 5 minutes in discussion.

And he said to them, "Take care, and be on your guard against all covetousness, for one's life does not consist in the abundance of his possessions." And he told them a parable, saying, "The land of a rich man produced plentifully, and he thought to himself, 'What shall I do, for I have nowhere to store my crops?' And he said, 'I will do this: I will tear down my barns and build larger ones, and there I will store all my grain and my goods. And I will say to my soul, "Soul, you have ample goods laid up for many years; relax, eat, drink, be merry."' But God said to him, 'Fool! This night your soul is required of you, and the things you have prepared, whose will they be?' So is the one who lays up treasure for himself and is not rich toward God."
Luke 12:15-21

▶ *What does it mean to be on guard against covetousness? What do you think Jesus means when he says "one's life does not consist in the abundance of his possessions"?*

Training Notes

Watch the video entitled "How Should We Steward Our Money?" found at *frontlinechurch.com/formation*. Use the notes below and fill in the blanks to follow along with the video.

...using money you haven't earned to buy things you don't need to impress people you don't like. **Robert Quillen,** *Detroit Free Press*

In his earthly ministry, Jesus constantly taught about money. Over 40% of his parables were about money and possessions.

——

For where your treasure is, there your heart will be also. **Matthew 6:21**

He even went so far as to describe money as a "god" competing for our worship, for our very hearts.

No one can serve two masters, for either he will hate the one and love the other, or he will be devoted to the one and despise the other. You cannot serve God and money. **Matthew 6:24**

Money as an ....

As for the rich in this present age, charge them not to be haughty, nor to set their hopes on the uncertainty of riches, but on God, who richly provides us with everything to enjoy. They are to do good, to be rich in good works, to be generous and ready to share, thus storing up treasure for themselves as a good foundation for the future, so that they may take hold of that which is truly life. **1 Timothy 6:17-19**

Even if we just have the basic necessities, we can be content and satisfied in God.

Now there is great gain in godliness with contentment, for we brought nothing into the world, and we cannot take anything out of the world. But if we have food and clothing, with these we will be content. **1 Timothy 6:6-8**

Money as a ....

It is more blessed to give than to receive. **Acts 20:35**

Early Christians were transformed by Jesus' teaching on money.

Do we not observe how the benevolence of Christians to strangers has done the most to advance their cause? It is disgraceful that [the Christians] support not only their poor but ours as well, while everyone is able to see that our own people lack aid from us. **Julian, *Letter to Arsacius***

As the Church, we should also be marked by lavish generosity towards one another.

Now the full number of those who believed were of one heart and soul, and no one said that any of the things that belonged to him was his own, but they had everything in common... There was not a needy person among them... **Acts 4:32, 34**

Money as a _____

> *Each one must give as he has decided in his heart, not reluctantly or under compulsion, for God loves a cheerful giver.* **2 Corinthians 9:7**

As we support the local church, we partner together to see our world transformed by the good news of Jesus.

> *For the ministry of this service is not only supplying the needs of the saints but is also overflowing in many thanksgivings to God. By their approval of this service, they will glorify God because of your submission that comes from your confession of the gospel of Christ, and the generosity of your contribution for them and for all others...* **2 Corinthians 9:12-13**

Ultimately, we'll move from consumerism to stewardship as we gaze upon the generosity of God.

> *For you know the grace of our Lord Jesus Christ, that though he was rich, yet for your sake he became poor, so that you by his poverty might become rich.* **2 Corinthians 8:9**

Discussion

Have two people read aloud the following two excerpts from "Greed" by David Mathis in *Killjoys: The Seven Deadly Sins,* and *The Treasure Principle* by Randy Alcorn. Then answer the accompanying discussion question.

David Mathis writes:

Each of us must wrestle personally with the fine line between healthy and unhealthy desires for possessions. While it might be unwise to prescribe particulars... it can be helpful to create general categories, and to describe errors to avoid.

One thing to note is that human life is not a static existence. God made us for rhythms and cadences, for feasting and fasting. There is benefit, even if minimal, in identifying and naming the extremes of sustained opulence, on the one hand, and austerity, on the other. We need a place for both financial feasting and fasting. We should abhor the so-called prosperity gospel, and not be fooled by loveless stinginess masquerading as Christian stewardship. However, while discerning from person to person precisely what's too little or too much is no easy task, [John] Piper wisely observes, "The impossibility of drawing a line between night and day doesn't mean you can't know it's midnight."

A final thing we might note here in terms of a practical standard is the test of sacrifice. Do you ever abstain from fulfilling your own sense of need in order to give to others? A life without the practice of sacrifice—a love that suffers want to meet the needs of others—is not a fully Christian life.

Randy Alcorn writes:

1. *God owns everything. I'm His money manager.*
   We are the managers of the assets God has entrusted to us.

2. *My heart always goes where I put God's money.*
   Watch what happens when you reallocate your money from temporal things to eternal things.

3. *Heaven, not earth, is my home.*
   We are citizens of "a better country—a heavenly one" (Heb 11:16).

4. *I should not live for the dot, but for the line.*
   From the dot—our present life on earth—extends a line that goes on forever, which is eternity in the new heavens and new earth (Rev 21:1–5).

5. *Giving is the only antidote to materialism.*
   Giving is a joyful surrender to a greater person and a greater agenda. It dethrones me and exalts God.

6. *God prospers me not to raise my standard of living, but to raise my standard of giving.*
   God gives us more money than we need so we can give generously.

▷ *While taking to heart the reminder that God calls us to both feasting and fasting, which of Alcorn's six principles is most convicting or reorienting for you, and why?*

Exercise

Take a few minutes to brainstorm ways you can expand your generosity as a group to meet needs in the city. Think of needs where you live, work, play, and study. No need is too big or too small.

Once completed, decide on at least one need to work towards meeting together. If financial assistance is needed, **Push Back Darkness Grants** are available. For more information, or to apply for a **Push Back Darkness Grant**, go to *frontlinechurch.com/grants*.

WHAT ARE THE NEEDS IN OUR COMMUNITY?

WHAT WOULD IT TAKE TO MEET THESE NEEDS?

LIST SPECIFIC ACTION STEPS AND ASSIGN PEOPLE TO EACH.

Benediction

To conclude your time, pray this prayer out loud together. The following is based on Ephesians 3:20-21.

Now to him who is able to do far more abundantly than all we could ask or think, according to the power at work within us—to him be glory in the Church and in Christ Jesus throughout all generations, forever and ever. *Amen.*

Joyful Generosity and the Local Church

A Take-Home Resource

The following is a brief resource on giving to the local church to read through on your own. Following the reading, there are questions to help you reflect on your giving. More information and resources can be found at *frontlinechurch.com/formation*.

As a response to God's gracious gift, followers of Jesus should commit to regular financial giving to the local church. The clear calling of Scripture is that financial giving and generosity isn't optional. In our giving, God is training us in righteousness and reshaping the way we understand money: as a gift, as a tool, and as an offering. An unwillingness to give and be honest in our sacrificial generosity is directly tied to the genuineness of our worship. To that end, we should think of giving to the local church in three primary categories:

Tithes

The word tithe comes from the Hebrew word "ma`aser," meaning "tenth." While tithing is an Old Testament financial principal, it is still a helpful model and starting place for the New Testament church. Tithes support the work of ministry, the spread of the gospel, and the establishment of bases for mission, both locally and globally. Followers of Jesus should commit to, or work toward, giving a regular tithe to their local church.

Alms

Alms are intentional gifts to the poor and most vulnerable in society. Throughout the Bible, God's heart is profoundly burdened for the poor and the marginalized. We should desire to make a felt impact on the social fabric where God has placed them. Churches may take up offerings especially designated to bring relief to the poor and distressed locally, nationally, and internationally.

Offerings

Offerings are gifts for specific needs. There are times when a church rallies around a specific gospel cause or need in their church, city, state, region, or another part of the world. As God opens up doors to serve and bless, churches should be able to joyfully and sacrificially respond with faith.

For a more in-depth look at what the Bible says about giving to the local church, read "Tithing, Giving, and Generosity" at *frontlinechurch.com/formation*.

Reflection Questions

▶ What percentage of your income are you currently giving to the local church? Is this where you want to be with your giving?

▶ Thinking about your generosity towards the local church, do you give "not reluctantly or under compulsion" but out of a "cheerful" heart (2 Cor 8:7)? Is your giving motivated by a desire to get God to bless you, or out of a pure and worshipful heart?

▶ If you would like to grow in your generosity to the church, brainstorm some ways you could make room in your budget for giving.

▶ If you need help with healthy budgeting and financial practices, who could you reach out to for help?

▶ Do you have any painful memories or experiences around giving and the local church? If so, have you had the opportunity to process those with someone safe and wise?

———

Stewards
of Possessions

Stewards of Possessions

——

Call to Worship

An invitation from God to all humanity to behold and join the story, work, and eternal worship of Jesus. This prayer is based on Psalm 50.

O God, you are the Mighty One who summons the riches of the earth with a word. The world and its fullness are yours. To you belong the cattle on a thousand hills, and even the sparrows rest in your care. You need no one and lack nothing, yet you command my praise—for your glory and for my joy. When my hands are full, fill me with gratitude. When my hands are empty, satisfy me with yourself. *Amen.*

Psalm 111

Praise the LORD!
I will give thanks to the LORD with my whole heart,
in the company of the upright, in the congregation.
Great are the works of the LORD,
studied by all who delight in them.
Full of splendor and majesty is his work,
and his righteousness endures forever.
He has caused his wondrous works to be remembered;
the LORD is gracious and merciful.
He provides food for those who fear him;
he remembers his covenant forever.
He has shown his people the power of his works,
in giving them the inheritance of the nations.
The works of his hands are faithful and just;
all his precepts are trustworthy;
they are established forever and ever,
to be performed with faithfulness and uprightness.
He sent redemption to his people;
he has commanded his covenant forever.
Holy and awesome is his name!
The fear of the LORD is the beginning of wisdom;
all those who practice it have a good understanding.
His praise endures forever!

Confession

A call to acknowledge and forsake sin against God and one another.

Jesus, you warned me, "Where your treasure is, there your heart will be also."

For all the ways I have given myself to the riches of this world—forgive me and bend my heart back to you.

For all the ways I have shut my eyes to the needs of the poor—open my hands to be generous like you.

For all the ways I have preferred your blessings over your presence—change me that I might enjoy your gifts and treasure you as Giver.

For all the ways I have looked to money as my security—save me from false refuges and help me to lean on you.

Silently reflect on the ways you have strayed from God's gracious authority. Confess aloud and receive God's free grace through Jesus.

Assurance

An invitation to receive the assurance of a new identity in the finished work of Christ.

Father, you are a generous Giver. There is no good thing that you withhold from me, for it is your good pleasure to give me the kingdom. You did not spare your own Son, but gave him up for us all. Surely you will graciously provide for my every need, both now and forever. If you are for me, who can be against me? You have given me the Spirit of adoption and called me your child. Who is there to condemn? Nothing in all creation will be able to separate me from your love. *Thanks be to God!*

Scripture Reading

The surrender to God's good and authoritative Word.

Someone in the crowd said to him, "Teacher, tell my brother to divide the inheritance with me." But he said to him, "Man, who made me a judge or arbitrator over you?" And he said to them, "Take care, and be on your guard against all covetousness, for one's life does not consist in the abundance of his possessions." And he told them a parable, saying, "The land of a rich man produced plentifully, and he thought to himself, What shall I do, for I have nowhere to store my crops?' And he said, 'I will do this: I will tear down my barns and build larger ones, and there I will store all my grain and my goods. And I will say to my soul, "Soul, you have ample goods laid up for many years; relax, eat, drink, be merry."' But God said to him, Fool! This night your soul is required of you, and the things you have prepared, whose will they be?' So is the one who lays up treasure for himself and is not rich toward God."

Luke 12:13-21

Prayer

An invitation to bring the needs of our bodies, hearts, and minds to the care of God.

Offer prayers for yourself and for others.

Benediction

A blessing from the authority of Scripture spoken over the people of God. The following is based on Philippians 4:19-20.

O my God, you will supply my every need according to your riches in glory in Christ Jesus. To you, Father, be glory forever and ever. *Send me now into the world as a steward of your good gifts.*

●＊＊＊＊

Stewards of Possessions

Call to Worship

An invitation from God to all humanity to behold and join the story, work, and eternal worship of Jesus. This prayer is based on James 1.

Father of lights, every good and perfect gift comes from you. Your generosity knows no bounds and never changes. In your grace, you gave me life by the Word of truth. Today I ask for wisdom to know how to live as a steward of your gifts— remembering that you give generously to all without reproach or reservation. *Amen.*

Psalm 116

I love the LORD, because he has heard
my voice and my pleas for mercy.
Because he inclined his ear to me,
therefore I will call on him as long as I live.
The snares of death encompassed me;
the pangs of Sheol laid hold on me;
I suffered distress and anguish.
Then I called on the name of the LORD:
"O LORD, I pray, deliver my soul!"

Gracious is the LORD, and righteous;
our God is merciful.
The LORD preserves the simple;
when I was brought low, he saved me.
Return, O my soul, to your rest;
for the LORD has dealt bountifully with you.

For you have delivered my soul from death,
my eyes from tears,
my feet from stumbling;
I will walk before the LORD
in the land of the living.

I believed, even when I spoke:
"I am greatly afflicted";
I said in my alarm,
"All mankind are liars."

What shall I render to the LORD
for all his benefits to me?
I will lift up the cup of salvation
and call on the name of the LORD,

I will pay my vows to the LORD
in the presence of all his people.

Precious in the sight of the LORD
is the death of his saints.
O LORD, I am your servant;
I am your servant, the son of your maidservant.
You have loosed my bonds.
I will offer to you the sacrifice of thanksgiving
and call on the name of the LORD.
I will pay my vows to the LORD
in the presence of all his people,
in the courts of the house of the LORD,
in your midst, O Jerusalem.
Praise the LORD!

Confession

A call to acknowledge and forsake sin against God and one another.

I hear your call to love you with all my heart, mind, and strength. But I confess that my love for you is diluted—made weak by lesser desires and a divided heart. *I have sought my own way, and my soul is unsatisfied.*

You have called me to steward your creation and fill it with blessing. But I have twisted your good gifts and turned them to my own ends. *I have sought my own way, and my soul is unsatisfied.*

Silently reflect on the ways you have strayed from God's gracious authority. Confess aloud and receive God's free grace through Jesus.

Assurance

An invitation to receive the assurance of a new identity in the finished work of Christ.

Father of lights, you richly give me all things to enjoy. In Jesus, I stand clothed in purity, washed in mercy, and adopted in love. I no longer have to leave the table of the world unsatisfied. You have spread a banquet before me filled with every good thing. Surely goodness and mercy will follow me all the days of my life, and I will find satisfaction in you. *Thanks be to God!*

Scripture Reading

The surrender to God's good and authoritative Word.

And he said to his disciples, "Therefore I tell you, do not be anxious about your life, what you will eat, nor about your body, what you will put on. For life is more than food, and the body more than clothing. Consider the ravens: they neither sow nor reap, they have neither storehouse nor barn, and yet God feeds them. Of how much more value are you than the birds! And which of you by being anxious can add a single hour to his span of life? If then you are not able to do as small a thing as that, why are you anxious about the rest? Consider the lilies, how they grow: they neither toil nor spin, yet I tell you, even Solomon in all his glory was not arrayed like one of these. But if God so clothes the grass, which is alive in the field today, and tomorrow is thrown into the oven, how much more will he clothe you, O you of little faith! And do not seek what you are to eat and what you are to drink, nor be worried. For all the nations of the world seek after these things, and your Father knows that you need them. Instead, seek his kingdom, and these things will be added to you.

"Fear not, little flock, for it is your Father's good pleasure to give you the kingdom. Sell your possessions, and give to the needy. Provide yourselves with moneybags that do not grow old, with a treasure in the heavens that does not fail, where no thief approaches and no moth destroys. For where your treasure is, there will your heart be also."

Luke 12:22-34

Prayer

An invitation to bring the needs of our bodies, hearts, and minds to the care of God.

Offer prayers for yourself and for others.

Benediction

A blessing from the authority of Scripture spoken over the people of God.
The following is based on Ephesians 3:20-21.

Now to him who is able to do far more abundantly than all I could ask or think, according to the power at work within me—to him be glory in the Church and in Christ Jesus throughout all generations, forever and ever. *Send me now into the world as a steward of your good gifts.*

Stewards of Possessions

―――

Call to Worship

An invitation from God to all humanity to behold and join the story, work, and eternal worship of Jesus. This prayer is based on Hebrews 2 and 4.

Jesus, you are a merciful and faithful high priest, crowned with glory and honor. You took my punishment, in my place, and graciously tasted death for me. You brought many sons and daughters to glory through suffering. Through death, you destroyed the one who has the power of death. Who am I that you are mindful of me and that you care for me? In this moment, give me confidence to draw near to your throne of grace, that I might receive the mercy and help I so desperately need. *Amen.*

Psalm 117

Praise the LORD, all nations!
Extol him, all peoples!
For great is his steadfast love toward us,
and the faithfulness of the LORD endures forever.
Praise the LORD!

Confession

A call to acknowledge and forsake sin against God and one another.

Jesus, you loved the unlovable. You feasted with the broken and the immoral. But I confess that, though I'm called to follow you, I often withdraw my presence and withhold my love from those around me. Father, forgive me. *I confess that I am not my own, but belong to you.*

Jesus, with all your strength, you sought to offer goodness to the world and glory to your Father. But I confess that I often withhold good from others and only seek to glorify myself. Father, forgive me. *I confess that I am not my own, but belong to you.*

Silently reflect on the ways you have strayed from God's gracious authority. Confess aloud and receive God's free grace through Jesus.

Assurance

An invitation to receive the assurance of a new identity in the finished work of Christ.

Lord, even though I have sinned against you, still you have loved me and given yourself for me. My old self went to the cross with Christ. And now it is no longer I who live, but Christ who lives in and through me. I am no longer my own, but I have been bought with an unspeakable price—your very blood. Your Spirit lives in me and leads me to lay aside my weak desires for the deeper delight of living for your glory. I have been made for you, I have been bought by you, and now I belong to you. *Thanks be to God!*

Scripture Reading

The surrender to God's good and authoritative Word.

He also said to the disciples, "There was a rich man who had a manager, and charges were brought to him that this man was wasting his possessions. And he called him and said to him, 'What is this that I hear about you? Turn in the account of your management, for you can no longer be manager.' And the manager said to himself, 'What shall I do, since my master is taking the management away from me? I am not strong enough to dig, and I am ashamed to beg. I have decided what to do, so that when I am removed from management, people may receive me into their houses.' So, summoning his master's debtors one by one, he said to the first, 'How much do you owe my master?' He said, 'A hundred measures of oil.' He said to him, 'Take your bill, and sit down quickly and write fifty.' Then he said to another, 'And how much do you owe?' He said, 'A hundred measures of wheat.' He said to him, 'Take your bill, and write eighty.' The master commended the dishonest manager for his shrewdness. For the sons of this world are more shrewd in dealing with their own generation than the sons of light. And I tell you, make friends for yourselves by means of unrighteous wealth, so that when it fails they may receive you into the eternal dwellings.

"One who is faithful in a very little is also faithful in much, and one who is dishonest in a very little is also dishonest in much. If then you have not been faithful in the unrighteous wealth, who will entrust to you the true riches? And if you have not been faithful in that which is another's, who will give you that which is your own? No servant can serve two masters, for either he will hate the one and love the other, or he will be devoted to the one and despise the other. You cannot serve God and money."

The Pharisees, who were lovers of money, heard all these things, and they ridiculed him. And he said to them, "You are those who justify yourselves before men, but God knows your hearts. For what is exalted among men is an abomination in the sight of God."

Luke 16:1-15

Prayer

An invitation to bring the needs of our bodies, hearts, and minds to the care of God.

Offer prayers for yourself and for others.

Benediction

A blessing from the authority of Scripture spoken over the people of God. The following is based on 2 Thessalonians 2:16-17.

Now may the Lord Jesus Christ himself, and God the Father, who loved me and gave me eternal comfort and good hope through grace, comfort my heart and establish it in every good work and word. *Send me now into the world as a steward of your good gifts.*

••••○○

Stewards of Possessions

———

Call to Worship

An invitation from God to all humanity to behold and join the story, work, and eternal worship of Jesus. This prayer is based on John 1.

Jesus, you are the Word of God. In the beginning, you were with God, and you were God. All things were made through you; nothing was made without you. You are life, and you bring light to our dark hearts. You took on flesh and dwelt among us so we might finally see and know the Father. Open my eyes to behold your glory, glory as of the only Son from the Father, full of grace and truth. *Amen.*

Psalm 125

A SONG OF ASCENTS.

Those who trust in the LORD are like Mount Zion,
which cannot be moved, but abides forever.
As the mountains surround Jerusalem,
so the LORD surrounds his people,
from this time forth and forevermore.
For the scepter of wickedness shall not rest
on the land allotted to the righteous,
lest the righteous stretch out
their hands to do wrong.
Do good, O LORD, to those who are good,
and to those who are upright in their hearts!
But those who turn aside to their crooked ways
the LORD will lead away with evildoers!
Peace be upon Israel!

Confession

A call to acknowledge and forsake sin against God and one another.

God of all grace, you have given me your Spirit and commissioned me as the aroma of Christ on earth. But I confess that I have taken your presence for granted and sought to satisfy my own cravings before looking to the needs of others. *Father, my heart is prone to wander.*

You have created me for relationship, but I have pulled away from my neighbors. I have lived like an island and pretended to be self-sufficient. I have believed the lie that it is more blessed to receive than to give. *Father, my heart is prone to wander.*

Silently reflect on the ways you have strayed from God's gracious authority. Confess aloud and receive God's free grace through Jesus.

•••••

Assurance

An invitation to receive the assurance of a new identity in the finished work of Christ.

While I was still a sinner, you died for me. Jesus, you were resurrected so I could know true and abundant life. While I have loved imperfectly, you have loved perfectly. While I have withheld myself from God and others, you have given yourself fully to the world. Lord, you intercede for me today, and you promise not to leave me as I am. Even now, you are at work to form me into your image, from one degree of glory to the next. You have not finished what you began in me, and you will not give up until it is done. *Thanks be to God!*

Scripture Reading

The surrender to God's good and authoritative Word.

And a ruler asked him, "Good Teacher, what must I do to inherit eternal life?" And Jesus said to him, "Why do you call me good? No one is good except God alone. You know the commandments: Do not commit adultery, Do not murder, Do not steal, Do not bear false witness, Honor your father and mother.'" And he said, "All these I have kept from my youth." When Jesus heard this, he said to him, "One thing you still lack. Sell all that you have and distribute to the poor, and you will have treasure in heaven; and come, follow me." But when he heard these things, he became very sad, for he was extremely rich. Jesus, seeing that he had become sad, said, "How difficult it is for those who have wealth to enter the kingdom of God! For it is easier for a camel to go through the eye of a needle than for a rich person to enter the kingdom of God." Those who heard it said, "Then who can be saved?" But he said, "What is impossible with man is possible with God." And Peter said, "See, we have left our homes and followed you." And he said to them, "Truly, I say to you, there is no one who has left house or wife or brothers or parents or children, for the sake of the kingdom of God, who will not receive many times more in this time, and in the age to come eternal life."

Luke 18:18-30

Prayer

An invitation to bring the needs of our bodies, hearts, and minds to the care of God.

Offer prayers for yourself and for others.

Benediction

A blessing from the authority of Scripture spoken over the people of God. The following is based on 2 Corinthians 13:14.

May the grace of the Lord Jesus, the love of God the Father, and the fellowship of the Holy Spirit go with me today. *Send me now into the world as a steward of your good gifts.*

Stewards of Possessions

——

Call to Worship

An invitation from God to all humanity to behold and join the story, work, and eternal worship of Jesus. This prayer is based on Psalm 50.

O God, you are the Mighty One who summons the riches of the earth with a word. The world and its fullness are yours. To you belong the cattle on a thousand hills, and even the sparrows rest in your care. You need no one and lack nothing, yet you command my praise—for your glory and for my joy. When my hands are full, fill me with gratitude. When my hands are empty, satisfy me with yourself. *Amen.*

Psalm 127

A SONG OF ASCENTS. OF SOLOMON.

Unless the LORD builds the house,
those who build it labor in vain.
Unless the LORD watches over the city,
the watchman stays awake in vain.
It is in vain that you rise up early
and go late to rest,
eating the bread of anxious toil;
for he gives to his beloved sleep.

Behold, children are a heritage from the LORD,
the fruit of the womb a reward.
Like arrows in the hand of a warrior
are the children of one's youth.
Blessed is the man
who fills his quiver with them!
He shall not be put to shame
when he speaks with his enemies in the gate.

Confession

A call to acknowledge and forsake sin against God and one another.

Jesus, you warned me, "Where your treasure is, there your heart will be also."

For all the ways I have given myself to the riches of this world—forgive me and bend my heart back to you.

For all the ways I have shut my eyes to the needs of the poor—open my hands to be generous like you.

•••••

For all the ways I have preferred your blessings over your presence—change me that I might enjoy your gifts and treasure you as Giver.

For all the ways I have looked to money as my security—save me from false refuges and help me to lean on you.

Silently reflect on the ways you have strayed from God's gracious authority. Confess aloud and receive God's free grace through Jesus.

Assurance

An invitation to receive the assurance of a new identity in the finished work of Christ.

Father, you are a generous Giver. There is no good thing that you withhold from me, for it is your good pleasure to give me the kingdom. You did not spare your own Son, but gave him up for us all. Surely you will graciously provide for my every need, both now and forever. If you are for me, who can be against me? You have given me the Spirit of adoption and called me your child. Who is there to condemn? Nothing in all creation will be able to separate me from your love. *Thanks be to God!*

Scripture Reading

The surrender to God's good and authoritative Word.

Now the full number of those who believed were of one heart and soul, and no one said that any of the things that belonged to him was his own, but they had everything in common. And with great power the apostles were giving their testimony to the resurrection of the Lord Jesus, and great grace was upon them all. There was not a needy person among them, for as many as were owners of lands or houses sold them and brought the proceeds of what was sold and laid it at the apostles' feet, and it was distributed to each as any had need. Thus Joseph, who was also called by the apostles Barnabas (which means son of encouragement), a Levite, a native of Cyprus, sold a field that belonged to him and brought the money and laid it at the apostles' feet.

Acts 4:32-37

Prayer

An invitation to bring the needs of our bodies, hearts, and minds to the care of God.

Offer prayers for yourself and for others.

•••••

Benediction

A blessing from the authority of Scripture spoken over the people of God.
The following is based on Philippians 4:19-20.

O my God, you will supply my every need according to your riches in glory in
Christ Jesus. To you, Father, be glory forever and ever. *Send me now into the world*
as a steward of your good gifts.

Daily Liturgies: Week 8

———

Stewards
of Possessions

Stewards of Possessions

____

Call to Worship

An invitation from God to all humanity to behold and join the story, work, and eternal worship of Jesus. This prayer is based on James 1.

Father of lights, every good and perfect gift comes from you. Your generosity knows no bounds and never changes. In your grace, you gave me life by the Word of truth. Today I ask for wisdom to know how to live as a steward of your gifts—remembering that you give generously to all without reproach or reservation. *Amen.*

Psalm 135:1-12

Praise the LORD!
Praise the name of the LORD,
give praise, O servants of the LORD,
who stand in the house of the LORD,
in the courts of the house of our God!
Praise the LORD, for the LORD is good;
sing to his name, for it is pleasant!
For the LORD has chosen Jacob for himself,
Israel as his own possession.

For I know that the LORD is great,
and that our Lord is above all gods.
Whatever the LORD pleases, he does,
in heaven and on earth,
in the seas and all deeps.
He it is who makes the clouds rise at the end of the earth,
who makes lightnings for the rain
and brings forth the wind from his storehouses.

He it was who struck down the firstborn of Egypt,
both of man and of beast;
who in your midst, O Egypt,
sent signs and wonders
against Pharaoh and all his servants;
who struck down many nations
and killed mighty kings,
Sihon, king of the Amorites,
and Og, king of Bashan,
and all the kingdoms of Canaan,
and gave their land as a heritage,
a heritage to his people Israel.

• • • • •

Confession

A call to acknowledge and forsake sin against God and one another.

I hear your call to love you with all my heart, mind, and strength. But I confess that my love for you is diluted—made weak by lesser desires and a divided heart. *I have sought my own way, and my soul is unsatisfied.*

You have called me to steward your creation and fill it with blessing. But I have twisted your good gifts and turned them to my own ends. *I have sought my own way, and my soul is unsatisfied.*

Silently reflect on the ways you have strayed from God's gracious authority. Confess aloud and receive God's free grace through Jesus.

Assurance

An invitation to receive the assurance of a new identity in the finished work of Christ.

Father of lights, you richly give me all things to enjoy. In Jesus, I stand clothed in purity, washed in mercy, and adopted in love. I no longer have to leave the table of the world unsatisfied. You have spread a banquet before me filled with every good thing. Surely goodness and mercy will follow me all the days of my life, and I will find satisfaction in you. *Thanks be to God!*

Scripture Reading

The surrender to God's good and authoritative Word.

If anyone teaches a different doctrine and does not agree with the sound words of our Lord Jesus Christ and the teaching that accords with godliness, he is puffed up with conceit and understands nothing. He has an unhealthy craving for controversy and for quarrels about words, which produce envy, dissension, slander, evil suspicions, and constant friction among people who are depraved in mind and deprived of the truth, imagining that godliness is a means of gain. But godliness with contentment is great gain, for we brought nothing into the world, and we cannot take anything out of the world. But if we have food and clothing, with these we will be content. But those who desire to be rich fall into temptation, into a snare, into many senseless and harmful desires that plunge people into ruin and destruction. For the love of money is a root of all kinds of evils. It is through this craving that some have wandered away from the faith and pierced themselves with many pangs.

1 Timothy 6:3-10

Prayer

An invitation to bring the needs of our bodies, hearts, and minds to the care of God.

Offer prayers for yourself and for others.

Benediction

A blessing from the authority of Scripture spoken over the people of God. The following is based on Ephesians 3:20-21.

Now to him who is able to do far more abundantly than all I could ask or think, according to the power at work within me—to him be glory in the Church and in Christ Jesus throughout all generations, forever and ever. *Send me now into the world as a steward of your good gifts.*

Stewards of Possessions

Call to Worship

An invitation from God to all humanity to behold and join the story, work, and eternal worship of Jesus. This prayer is based on Hebrews 2 and 4.

Jesus, you are a merciful and faithful high priest, crowned with glory and honor. You took my punishment, in my place, and graciously tasted death for me. You brought many sons and daughters to glory through suffering. Through death, you destroyed the one who has the power of death. Who am I that you are mindful of me and that you care for me? In this moment, give me confidence to draw near to your throne of grace, that I might receive the mercy and help I so desperately need. *Amen.*

Psalm 135:13-21

Your name, O LORD, endures forever,
your renown, O LORD, throughout all ages.
For the LORD will vindicate his people
and have compassion on his servants.

The idols of the nations are silver and gold,
the work of human hands.
They have mouths, but do not speak;
they have eyes, but do not see;
they have ears, but do not hear,
nor is there any breath in their mouths.
Those who make them become like them,
so do all who trust in them.

O house of Israel, bless the LORD!
O house of Aaron, bless the LORD!
O house of Levi, bless the LORD!
You who fear the LORD, bless the LORD!
Blessed be the LORD from Zion,
he who dwells in Jerusalem!
Praise the LORD!

Confession

A call to acknowledge and forsake sin against God and one another.

Jesus, you loved the unlovable. You feasted with the broken and the immoral. But I confess that, though I'm called to follow you, I often withdraw my presence and withhold my love from those around me. Father, forgive me. *I confess that I am not my own, but belong to you.*

Jesus, with all your strength, you sought to offer goodness to the world and glory to your Father. But I confess that I often withhold good from others and only seek to glorify myself. Father, forgive me. *I confess that I am not my own, but belong to you.*

Silently reflect on the ways you have strayed from God's gracious authority. Confess aloud and receive God's free grace through Jesus.

Assurance

An invitation to receive the assurance of a new identity in the finished work of Christ.

Lord, even though I have sinned against you, still you have loved me and given yourself for me. My old self went to the cross with Christ. And now it is no longer I who live, but Christ who lives in and through me. I am no longer my own, but I have been bought with an unspeakable price—your very blood. Your Spirit lives in me and leads me to lay aside my weak desires for the deeper delight of living for your glory. I have been made for you, I have been bought by you, and now I belong to you. *Thanks be to God!*

Scripture Reading

The surrender to God's good and authoritative Word.

But as for you, O man of God, flee these things. Pursue righteousness, godliness, faith, love, steadfastness, gentleness. Fight the good fight of the faith. Take hold of the eternal life to which you were called and about which you made the good confession in the presence of many witnesses. I charge you in the presence of God, who gives life to all things, and of Christ Jesus, who in his testimony before Pontius Pilate made the good confession, to keep the commandment unstained and free from reproach until the appearing of our Lord Jesus Christ, which he will display at the proper time—he who is the blessed and only Sovereign, the King of kings and Lord of lords, who alone has immortality, who dwells in unapproachable light, whom no one has ever seen or can see. To him be honor and eternal dominion. Amen.

As for the rich in this present age, charge them not to be haughty, nor to set their hopes on the uncertainty of riches, but on God, who richly provides us with everything to enjoy. They are to do good, to be rich in good works, to be generous and ready to share, thus storing up treasure for themselves as a good foundation for the future, so that they may take hold of that which is truly life.

————

O Timothy, guard the deposit entrusted to you. Avoid the irreverent babble and contradictions of what is falsely called "knowledge," for by professing it some have swerved from the faith.

Grace be with you.

1 Timothy 6:11-21

Prayer

An invitation to bring the needs of our bodies, hearts, and minds to the care of God.

Offer prayers for yourself and for others.

Benediction

A blessing from the authority of Scripture spoken over the people of God.
The following is based on 2 Thessalonians 2:16-17.

Now may the Lord Jesus Christ himself, and God the Father, who loved me and gave me eternal comfort and good hope through grace, comfort my heart and establish it in every good work and word. *Send me now into the world as a steward of your good gifts.*

Stewards of Possessions

———

Call to Worship

An invitation from God to all humanity to behold and join the story, work, and eternal worship of Jesus. This prayer is based on John 1.

Jesus, you are the Word of God. In the beginning, you were with God, and you were God. All things were made through you; nothing was made without you. You are life, and you bring light to our dark hearts. You took on flesh and dwelt among us so we might finally see and know the Father. Open my eyes to behold your glory, glory as of the only Son from the Father, full of grace and truth. *Amen.*

Psalm 138

OF DAVID.

I give you thanks, O LORD, with my whole heart;
before the gods I sing your praise;
I bow down toward your holy temple
and give thanks to your name for your steadfast love and your faithfulness,
for you have exalted above all things
your name and your word.
On the day I called, you answered me;
my strength of soul you increased.

All the kings of the earth shall give you thanks, O LORD,
for they have heard the words of your mouth,
and they shall sing of the ways of the LORD,
for great is the glory of the LORD.
For though the LORD is high, he regards the lowly,
but the haughty he knows from afar.

Though I walk in the midst of trouble,
you preserve my life;
you stretch out your hand against the wrath of my enemies,
and your right hand delivers me.
The LORD will fulfill his purpose for me;
your steadfast love, O LORD, endures forever.
Do not forsake the work of your hands.

••••••

Confession

A call to acknowledge and forsake sin against God and one another.

God of all grace, you have given me your Spirit and commissioned me as the aroma of Christ on earth. But I confess that I have taken your presence for granted and sought to satisfy my own cravings before looking to the needs of others. *Father, my heart is prone to wander.*

You have created me for relationship, but I have pulled away from my neighbors. I have lived like an island and pretended to be self-sufficient. I have believed the lie that it is more blessed to receive than to give. *Father, my heart is prone to wander.*

Silently reflect on the ways you have strayed from God's gracious authority. Confess aloud and receive God's free grace through Jesus.

Assurance

An invitation to receive the assurance of a new identity in the finished work of Christ.

While I was still a sinner, you died for me. Jesus, you were resurrected so I could know true and abundant life. While I have loved imperfectly, you have loved perfectly. While I have withheld myself from God and others, you have given yourself fully to the world. Lord, you intercede for me today, and you promise not to leave me as I am. Even now, you are at work to form me into your image, from one degree of glory to the next. You have not finished what you began in me, and you will not give up until it is done. *Thanks be to God!*

Scripture Reading

The surrender to God's good and authoritative Word.

We want you to know, brothers, about the grace of God that has been given among the churches of Macedonia, for in a severe test of affliction, their abundance of joy and their extreme poverty have overflowed in a wealth of generosity on their part. For they gave according to their means, as I can testify, and beyond their means, of their own accord, begging us earnestly for the favor of taking part in the relief of the saints— and this, not as we expected, but they gave themselves first to the Lord and then by the will of God to us. Accordingly, we urged Titus that as he had started, so he should complete among you this of grace. But as you excel in everything—in faith, in speech, in knowledge, in all earnestness, and in our love for you—see that you excel in this act of grace also.

I say this not as a command, but to prove by the earnestness of others that your love also is genuine. For you know the grace of our Lord Jesus Christ, that though he was rich, yet for your sake he became poor, so that you by his poverty might

_____

become rich. And in this matter I give my judgment: this benefits you, who a year ago started not only to do this work but also to desire to do it. So now finish doing it as well, so that your readiness in desiring it may be matched by your completing it out of what you have. For if the readiness is there, it is acceptable according to what a person has, not according to what he does not have. For I do not mean that others should be eased and you burdened, but that as a matter of fairness your abundance at the present time should supply their need, so that their abundance may supply your need, that there may be fairness. As it is written, "Whoever gathered much had nothing left over, and whoever gathered little had no lack."

2 Corinthians 8:1-15

Prayer

An invitation to bring the needs of our bodies, hearts, and minds to the care of God.

Offer prayers for yourself and for others.

Benediction

A blessing from the authority of Scripture spoken over the people of God. The following is based on 2 Corinthians 13:14.

May the grace of the Lord Jesus, the love of God the Father, and the fellowship of the Holy Spirit go with me today. *Send me now into the world as a steward of your good gifts.*

Stewards of Possessions

___

Call to Worship

An invitation from God to all humanity to behold and join the story, work, and eternal worship of Jesus. This prayer is based on Psalm 50.

O God, you are the Mighty One who summons the riches of the earth with a word. The world and its fullness are yours. To you belong the cattle on a thousand hills, and even the sparrows rest in your care. You need no one and lack nothing, yet you command my praise—for your glory and for my joy. When my hands are full, fill me with gratitude. When my hands are empty, satisfy me with yourself. *Amen.*

Psalm 144

OF DAVID.

Blessed be the LORD, my rock,
who trains my hands for war,
and my fingers for battle;
he is my steadfast love and my fortress,
my stronghold and my deliverer,
my shield and he in whom I take refuge,
who subdues peoples under me.

O LORD, what is man that you regard him,
or the son of man that you think of him?
Man is like a breath;
his days are like a passing shadow.

Bow your heavens, O LORD, and come down!
Touch the mountains so that they smoke!
Flash forth the lightning and scatter them;
send out your arrows and rout them!
Stretch out your hand from on high;
rescue me and deliver me from the many waters,
from the hand of foreigners,
whose mouths speak lies
and whose right hand is a right hand of falsehood.

I will sing a new song to you, O God;
upon a ten-stringed harp I will play to you,
who gives victory to kings,
who rescues David his servant from the cruel sword.
Rescue me and deliver me
from the hand of foreigners,

•••••

whose mouths speak lies
and whose right hand is a right hand of falsehood.

May our sons in their youth
be like plants full grown,
our daughters like corner pillars
cut for the structure of a palace;
may our granaries be full,
providing all kinds of produce;
may our sheep bring forth thousands
and ten thousands in our fields;
may our cattle be heavy with young,
suffering no mishap or failure in bearing;
may there be no cry of distress in our streets!
Blessed are the people to whom such blessings fall!
Blessed are the people whose God is the LORD!

Confession

A call to acknowledge and forsake sin against God and one another.

Jesus, you warned me, "Where your treasure is, there your heart will be also."

For all the ways I have given myself to the riches of this world—forgive me and bend my heart back to you.

For all the ways I have shut my eyes to the needs of the poor—open my hands to be generous like you.

For all the ways I have preferred your blessings over your presence—change me that I might enjoy your gifts and treasure you as Giver.

For all the ways I have looked to money as my security—save me from false refuges and help me to lean on you.

Silently reflect on the ways you have strayed from God's gracious authority. Confess aloud and receive God's free grace through Jesus.

Assurance

An invitation to receive the assurance of a new identity in the finished work of Christ.

Father, you are a generous Giver. There is no good thing that you withhold from me, for it is your good pleasure to give me the kingdom. You did not spare your own Son, but gave him up for us all. Surely you will graciously provide for my every need, both now and forever. If you are for me, who can be against me?

———

You have given me the Spirit of adoption and called me your child. Who is there to condemn? Nothing in all creation will be able to separate me from your love. *Thanks be to God!*

Scripture Reading

The surrender to God's good and authoritative Word.

But thanks be to God, who put into the heart of Titus the same earnest care I have for you. For he not only accepted our appeal, but being himself very earnest he is going to you of his own accord. With him we are sending the brother who is famous among all the churches for his preaching of the gospel. And not only that, but he has been appointed by the churches to travel with us as we carry out this act of grace that is being ministered by us, for the glory of the Lord himself and to show our good will. We take this course so that no one should blame us about this generous gift that is being administered by us, for we aim at what is honorable not only in the Lord's sight but also in the sight of man. And with them we are sending our brother whom we have often tested and found earnest in many matters, but who is now more earnest than ever because of his great confidence in you. As for Titus, he is my partner and fellow worker for your benefit. And as for our brothers, they are messengers of the churches, the glory of Christ. So give proof before the churches of your love and of our boasting about you to these men.

2 Corinthians 8:16-24

Prayer

An invitation to bring the needs of our bodies, hearts, and minds to the care of God.

Offer prayers for yourself and for others.

Benediction

A blessing from the authority of Scripture spoken over the people of God. The following is based on Philippians 4:19-20.

O my God, you will supply my every need according to your riches in glory in Christ Jesus. To you, Father, be glory forever and ever. *Send me now into the world as a steward of your good gifts.*

Stewards of Possessions

Call to Worship

An invitation from God to all humanity to behold and join the story, work, and eternal worship of Jesus. This prayer is based on James 1.

Father of lights, every good and perfect gift comes from you. Your generosity knows no bounds and never changes. In your grace, you gave me life by the Word of truth. Today I ask for wisdom to know how to live as a steward of your gifts—remembering that you give generously to all without reproach or reservation. *Amen.*

Psalm 146

Praise the LORD!
Praise the LORD, O my soul!
I will praise the LORD as long as I live;
I will sing praises to my God while I have my being.

Put not your trust in princes,
in a son of man, in whom there is no salvation.
When his breath departs, he returns to the earth;
on that very day his plans perish.

Blessed is he whose help is the God of Jacob,
whose hope is in the LORD his God,
who made heaven and earth,
the sea, and all that is in them,
who keeps faith forever;
who executes justice for the oppressed,
who gives food to the hungry.

The LORD sets the prisoners free;
the LORD opens the eyes of the blind.
The LORD lifts up those who are bowed down;
the LORD loves the righteous.
The LORD watches over the sojourners;
he upholds the widow and the fatherless,
but the way of the wicked he brings to ruin.

The LORD will reign forever,
your God, O Zion, to all generations.
Praise the LORD!

Confession

A call to acknowledge and forsake sin against God and one another.

I hear your call to love you with all my heart, mind, and strength. But I confess that my love for you is diluted—made weak by lesser desires and a divided heart. *I have sought my own way, and my soul is unsatisfied.*

You have called me to steward your creation and fill it with blessing. But I have twisted your good gifts and turned them to my own ends. *I have sought my own way, and my soul is unsatisfied.*

Silently reflect on the ways you have strayed from God's gracious authority. Confess aloud and receive God's free grace through Jesus.

Assurance

An invitation to receive the assurance of a new identity in the finished work of Christ.

Father of lights, you richly give me all things to enjoy. In Jesus, I stand clothed in purity, washed in mercy, and adopted in love. I no longer have to leave the table of the world unsatisfied. You have spread a banquet before me filled with every good thing. Surely goodness and mercy will follow me all the days of my life, and I will find satisfaction in you. *Thanks be to God!*

Scripture Reading

The surrender to God's good and authoritative Word.

Now it is superfluous for me to write to you about the ministry for the saints, for I know your readiness, of which I boast about you to the people of Macedonia, saying that Achaia has been ready since last year. And your zeal has stirred up most of them. But I am sending the brothers so that our boasting about you may not prove empty in this matter, so that you may be ready, as I said you would be. Otherwise, if some Macedonians come with me and find that you are not ready, we would be humiliated—to say nothing of you—for being so confident. So I thought it necessary to urge the brothers to go on ahead to you and arrange in advance for the gift you have promised, so that it may be ready as a willing gift, not as an exaction.

The point is this: whoever sows sparingly will also reap sparingly, and whoever sows bountifully will also reap bountifully. Each one must give as he has decided in his heart, not reluctantly or under compulsion, for God loves a cheerful giver. And God is able to make all grace abound to you, so that having all sufficiency in all things at all times, you may abound in every good work. As it is written,

•••••

"He has distributed freely, he has given to the poor;
his righteousness endures forever."

He who supplies seed to the sower and bread for food will supply and multiply your seed for sowing and increase the harvest of your righteousness. You will be enriched in every way to be generous in every way, which through us will produce thanksgiving to God. For the ministry of this service is not only supplying the needs of the saints but is also overflowing in many thanksgivings to God. By their approval of this service, they will glorify God because of your submission that comes from your confession of the gospel of Christ, and the generosity of your contribution for them and for all others, while they long for you and pray for you, because of the surpassing grace of God upon you. Thanks be to God for his inexpressible gift!

2 Corinthians 9:1-15

Prayer

An invitation to bring the needs of our bodies, hearts, and minds to the care of God.

Offer prayers for yourself and for others.

Benediction

*A blessing from the authority of Scripture spoken over the people of God.
The following is based on Ephesians 3:20-21.*

Now to him who is able to do far more abundantly than all I could ask or think, according to the power at work within me—to him be glory in the Church and in Christ Jesus throughout all generations, forever and ever. *Send me now into the world as a steward of your good gifts.*

•••••

Made in the USA
Coppell, TX
03 October 2022

83982901R00122